CÉZANNE'S

TEXT AND PHOTOGRAPHY BY

Derek Fell

GARDEN

SIMON & SCHUSTER

NEW YORK   LONDON   TORONTO   SYDNEY   SINGAPORE

SIMON & SCHUSTER
Rockefeller Center
1230 Avenue of the Americas
New York, NY 10020

SIMON & SCHUSTER and colophon are registered
trademarks of Simon & Schuster, Inc.

For information about special discounts for bulk purchases,
please contact Simon & Schuster Special Sales at
1-800-456-6798 or business@simonandschuster.com

Designed by Amy Hill,
based on a design by Jim Wageman, Wigwag

Manufactured in China

10 9 8 7 6 5 4 3 2 1

Library of Congress Cataloging-in-Publication Data
Fell, Derek.
  Cézanne's garden text and photography by Derek Fell.
    p. cm.
  Includes index.
  1. Cézanne, Paul, 1839–1906—Criticism and interpretation.
  2. Cézanne, Paul, 1839–1906—Homes and haunts—France—
  Aix-en-Provence. 3. Gardens in art. 4. Gardens—France—
  Aix-en-Provence—Design. I. Title.
  ND553.C33F395 2003
  759.4—dc22   2003059110

ISBN 0-7432-2536-8

TO THE MEMORY OF PAUL CÉZANNE (1839–1906)

Paul Cézanne *with one of his* Bathers *paintings.*

acknowledgments

OPPOSITE

Judas tree, also known as redbud, shading Cézanne's courtyard.

Cézanne's Garden is like no other garden . . . it has escaped all intentions except those of nature. . . . Like some of the most beautiful gardens of the world, Cézanne's Garden survives only through nature.

— MARIANNE R. BOURGES, *LE JARDIN DE CÉZANNE*, 1984

IN MY QUEST TO UNDERSTAND Cézanne's garden philosophy—an endeavor that has spanned more than ten years—there are many people I need to thank. First my wife, Carolyn, who accompanied me on my initial visit to Cézanne's Garden, Les Lauves, and who provided encouragement to see the project completed. Thanks also to Michel Colas, former director of tourism for the Côte d'Azur, who first invited me to Provence to photograph the gardens of Cézanne and Renoir.

At the Cézanne Museum, both Michel Fraisset (curator) and Catherine Cazin (interpreter of Cézanne's life and oeuvre) provided a great deal of information concerning Cézanne's studio and restored garden.

Four earlier books about Impressionist painters and their gardens preceded this work about Cézanne. They were *Renoir's Garden* and *The Impressionist Garden* (Frances Lincoln), *Secrets of Monet's Garden* (Friedman/Fairfax), and *Van Gogh's Gardens* (Simon & Schuster). Research into each of these gave me valuable insights into Cézanne's world.

I value the encouragement and advice of Albert Zuckerman, my literary agent, in recognizing the need for a book about Cézanne's garden, and of my editor at Simon & Schuster, Amanda Murray, in helping with the outline and bringing to the project a team of talented people.

Entrance to Cézanne's studio, the front door framed by vigorous growth of wild rosemary and fruiting fig.

Cézanne's Garden

CÉZANNE'S LOVE OF GARDENS

Nature is not on the surface; it is in the depths. Colors are the surface expression of the depth. They grow up from the roots of the world. They are its life, the life of ideas.

— CÉZANNE EXPLAINING HIS ARTISTIC RESPONSE TO NATURE

Pots of geraniums displayed on a block of limestone at the edge of Cézanne's courtyard.

PAUL CÉZANNE (1839–1906) was born into a wealthy family living at Aix-en-Provence, in the south of France. He left Aix at intervals for Paris in search of artistic development, but he was drawn back to his home by the strong colors of the surrounding countryside, the intensity of the light, and the dynamics of a mountainous landscape within sight of the ancient fortified city.

Though Cézanne disappointed his father, a banker, by choosing painting as a profession, his father granted him a small monthly allowance to pursue his ambition. Until his mid-fifties, however, Cézanne's sales were few, and he did not feel financially secure until his parents died, leaving him a sizeable inheritance and the means to build his own studio and garden on the outskirts of town.

Cézanne's early work was somber, but after meeting members of the Impressionist movement in Paris, he adopted a palette of lighter tones. Under the tutelage of Camille Pissarro, the eldest of ten painters who established the Impressionist movement, Cézanne worked doggedly at capturing the landscape in a way that expressed his innermost response to nature. He then moved beyond Impressionism to depict form with paint in a structural way, using blocky brushstrokes and flat expanses of color to diminish the sensation of perspective. This led him, in his final years, to experiment with abstraction. His revolutionary style was admired by such contemporaries as Claude Monet, Pierre-Auguste Renoir, and Paul Gauguin; it influenced subsequent painters including Pablo

Picasso, Georges Braque, and Henri Matisse when they began to explore more modernistic forms of artistic expression such as cubism.

After Cézanne's death a virtual stampede of early-twentieth-century artists descended on Provence, not only Picasso, Braque, and Matisse, but Dufy, Derain, Chagall, Soutine, Modigliani, Bonnard, and Signac, establishing Cézanne firmly as "the father of modern art."

This book examines an aspect of Cézanne's life that has received scant attention—his garden philosophy. Beginning with a look at the garden he painted when he lived on the family estate, the Jas de Bouffan (House of the Winds), the book also explains Cézanne's particular fascination with the garden of the nearby Château Noir, a property he tried to acquire when the Jas de Bouffan was sold. Most important, the book focuses on the garden of Les Lauves, which Cézanne created during the last five years of his life, when he made a studio and secluded garden on a half acre of sloping farmland on the edge of town.

Entrance to Cézanne's studio from the
woodland garden.

Courtyard, Les Lauves, with petunias clustered in clay pots, and spires of acanthus below the window.

Every morning, Cézanne would leave the apartment he shared with his wife in town. Invariably dressed in a dark three-piece suit and a black bowler, he presented an odd appearance, with bulging eyes and a goatee. He would climb the steep hill to Les Lauves, enter his walled sanctuary through solid puce-colored carriage doors, and cross a gravel courtyard to the studio for his painting paraphernalia. On rainy days he would work in the upstairs studio, but on a fine day he might choose a motif in the garden or the surrounding countryside. Even his gardener, Vallier, a dignified gentleman in a panama hat, became a favorite subject.

Though relatively modest in scale, the garden offered endless artistic possibilities, for even the smallest tracery of branches and leaves could command Cézanne's interest. He was a staunch conservationist, and nature's triumph over man's dominion was one of his favorite themes and the key to an understanding of his garden philosophy. "Art must make Nature eternal in our imagination," he once wrote.

Today the studio and restored garden of Les Lauves is visited by nearly a hundred thousand people a year. It is not as famous as Monet's colorful flower garden near Paris nor as spacious as Renoir's rose garden and wildflower meadow near Nice, but it is both evocative of Cézanne's art and illuminating of the reason for his greatness.

More than those of any other painter, Cézanne's explorations into artistic technique justify a reputation that inspired the French government to place his portrait on its most frequently used currency, the hundred-franc note, before France adopted the euro as currency.

CHAPTER ONE

CÉZANNE'S EARLY GARDENS:

THE JAS DE BOUFFAN AND CHÂTEAU NOIR

The artist learns to paint from the great masters;
he learns to see from nature.

—CÉZANNE, WRITING TO ARTIST EMILE BERNARD

OPPOSITE

Main driveway to the Jas de Bouffan,
with old sycamore trees (also known as
buttonwoods) and a border of bearded iris
casting shadows across the drive and lawn.

ART HISTORIANS consider Cézanne a post-Impressionist painter because he embraced the controversial art movement after its inception. Among the principal proponents of Impressionism were Monet and Renoir, Mary Cassatt and Berthe Morisot. Cézanne later declared his separation from the movement because he believed the Impressionists sought fleeting moments of sunlight and shadow and captured mostly ephemeral reflective lighting effects. As Cézanne's art matured, he considered Impressio*nist paintings anemic. He developed a style that instead sought to portray nature's structure, solidity, and strength, emphasizing its empirical geometry. In nature's shapes he saw variations of the cylinder, the cone, and the sphere. He eventually called Impressionism "the Sunday celebration of the moment," and he began to portray the permanence of nature in a bolder, more distinctive style. "I proceed very slowly, for nature reveals herself to me in very complex form and constant progress must be made. One must express oneself with distinction and strength," he wrote.

Even though Cézanne enjoyed painting *en plein air,* directly from nature, he needed a studio in which to finish off his outdoor studies and to paint still lifes during inclement weather. His first studio in Aix was a room provided by his father at the Jas de Bouffan. It was a convenient arrangement, considering that the large parklike garden surrounding the house was full of interesting subjects to paint.

The year 1897 marked the most disturbing emotional event in Cézanne's life—the loss of his mother. The event affected him not only psychologically but also physically, for her death forced the sale of the family's estate in order to settle a substantial inheritance the artist shared with his two younger sisters.

Approaching sixty years of age, Cézanne had grown fond of the old house and its somber grounds. He deplored the idea of suddenly pulling himself up by the roots and detaching himself from a property to which his art and life had been anchored for thirty-seven years. He was a man steeped in conservative habits, resentful of the slightest change in his surroundings, and suspicious of all new faces and modern inventions, such as gaslight and electricity.

THE JAS DE BOUFFAN

Cézanne's family home, the Jas de Bouffan, was an important early motif, particularly its eerie, mature garden of old trees and dark, formal reflecting pool. On its spacious, austere grounds Cézanne produced thirty-nine oils and seventeen watercolors. The thirty-four-acre (fourteen hectares) estate was purchased by Cézanne's father, Louis-Auguste Cézanne, in 1859, and it served as Cézanne's home until 1899, when he and his two sisters sold it to Louis Granel, an agronomic engineer. Following Granel's death, the property passed to his grandson, the late Dr. Frederic Corsy, who sold it to the city of Aix in 1994.

CÉZANNE'S EARLY GARDENS: THE JAS DE BOUFFAN AND CHÂTEAU NOIR

Paul Cézanne, Chestnut Trees at the Jas de Bouffan; *The Minneapolis Institute of Arts. These trees still stand, along a path at the rear of the main residence.*

Avenue of sycamore trees lining the main driveway of the Jas de Bouffan.

Eventually, the city intends to open it to the public as a museum.

Today at Aix it's possible to look through the wrought-iron gates of the mysterious Jas de Bouffan and see its gloomy, ivy-covered façade framed by an immense avenue of sycamore trees underplanted with blue irises. The three-story house has a red pantiled roof, beige walls set with tall, arched windows, and blue shutters. One painting, entitled *Jas de Bouffan* (1885–87), shows the mansion at the end of a sunlit lawn, a snaking garden wall leading the eye past a Provençal farmhouse and across the front of the main house. The farmhouse appears to stand next to the main residence, but this proximity of the two buildings unobscured by trees is a deliberate exaggeration. Although the estate featured several tenant farmhouses, none was so close to the main residence. Cézanne's telescoping of the distances allows him to show the contrast in geometric architectural elements between the dignified elegance of the main building and the more spartan lines of the farmhouse. Both structures are slightly inclined to the left, a favorite distortion to establish Cézanne's perception of equilibrium.

Cézanne painted the main house and the garden from numerous vantage points, and usually framed the house with tall trees. *Pool at the Jas de Bouffan* (1885–90) is Cézanne's most alluring image of the garden itself, for it shows the atmosphere of the garden without buildings. An elevated reflecting pool appears at one end, topped by a wrought-iron railing of a type used in cemeteries. The pool actually served as a reservoir. Below

the pool wall is what appears to be a gravestone: it is actually a wall fountain with a basin for washing laundry. Flanking the pool, and adding to the sinister graveyard atmosphere, is a crouching lion sculpture, its hindquarters raised in the air. The massive trunks of two chestnut trees rise above the pool in the foreground, their pendulous leafy branches providing a shadowy contrast to a sunlit mountain in the distance.

Another painting of the reflecting pool, *The Lake at the Jas de Bouffan* (1885), shows the heavily shaded pool again looking cemetery-like, with bright pink flowers of a red shrub hydrangea piercing the gloomy atmosphere.

The estate occupies a low-lying plain that is today hemmed in on all sides by traffic congestion and development, intensifying the sad, monastic, oppressive atmosphere of the place.

When Renoir visited Cézanne in the winter of 1888 and was offered a room in the house, he found its interior so unsettling that after one night he fled "the dark miserliness that fills the house" and accepted more comfortable lodgings with Cézanne's sister Rose.

Nevertheless, Cézanne was sorry to lose the Jas de Bouffan, and his first inclination was to try to replace it with an equally sinister dwelling and austere garden, the Château Noir (Black Castle), which also became a favorite subject.

THE CHÂTEAU NOIR

The subject of nineteen oils and twenty watercolors, the Château Noir is situated on a steep, rocky slope along the route du Tholonet. Veiled by tall trees, its topmost floor provides spectacular views of Mont Sainte-Victoire. The property was owned by an eccentric coal merchant, who is said to have painted the interior walls and furniture black. The garden had a brooding atmosphere, with trees and shrubs growing tortuously out of grotesque rock formations. The neo-Gothic house itself, unfinished, was made all the more ghostly by a row of columns intended to support an orangerie that was never completed. The once formal terraced gardens had begun to revert to wilderness. Cézanne loved the place for its wild, oppressive appearance, nature reclaiming man's dominion— "a virtually inexhaustible source of motifs," according to art historian Evmarie Schmitt, who also expressed the opinion that Cézanne was fascinated with its mystical aura, an aura he emphasized in his paintings.

Cézanne painted its courtyard with an

OPPOSITE

Close-up of the mottled bark of the sycamore trees lining the Jas de Bouffan driveway, many of the trunks garlanded with English ivy.

BELOW

Oval driveway of the Jas de Bouffan, with ivy-covered monument in the middle of the lawn.

13

ancient, gnarled pistachio tree uprooting its
stonework and threatening to tear the fabric of
the house itself apart. He painted the property's
tree-canopied, crumbling terraces, its unfinished balustrades, wellheads, and cisterns, ivy-
cloaked tree trunks silhouetted against sheer
cliff sides, and the tracery of shadows cast onto
the bare stone.

Cézanne's most interesting painting of the
garden at the Château Noir, *Millstone and Cistern
Under Trees* (1892), shows piles of quarry stones,
stone columns, and a millstone stockpiled in the
woods, waiting to be used in the construction
of the garden terraces. As recently as 1935 the
pile of landscape material was still there, almost
submerged in undergrowth. All Cézanne's favorite geometric shapes are represented in the
painting—the sphere by the millstone, the cylinder by the cistern, and the cone by intersect-
ing branches from saplings growing through the
piles of stone.

Cézanne at first rented a room off the courtyard at the Château Noir to store his work in
progress, and after the sale of the Jas de Bouffan, he tried to purchase the property outright
but could not come to terms with the owner.
Thwarted in his attempt to buy a ready-made
home and mature wild garden, he settled on
creating his own concept of paradise at Les
Lauves, a property equidistant from the Jas de
Bouffan and the Château Noir. This half acre
of ground won his heart because it was close to
his favorite outdoor motifs, especially his beloved mountain and the garden in decline at the
Château Noir. Cézanne filled Les Lauves with
many enduring natural elements: the organic

structural silhouettes of branches, vines, and tree trunks; the billowing, vibrating forms of foliage; the solidity of fieldstone walls, stone steps, benches, and stone terraces. Within a short motor ride were myriad scenic views to paint: groves of splendid umbrella pines with radiating arms; gravel tracks leading through farmland; meadows; woodland; and weather-worn rock escarpments at the base of his revered mountain, Mont Sainte-Victoire. The location was perfect—a walled space to create a secluded naturalistic garden like no other, and beyond its walls a natural landscape unmatched anywhere in France.

Les Lauves had sloping terrain similar to the Château Noir's, but it had a sunnier aspect. Cézanne immediately set about making terraces like those at the château, hauling to the site large limestone blocks to serve as pedestals for plants in terra-cotta urns. Within five years of purchasing the property, he had succeeded in creating a haven of contentment, with splendid views of Aix downhill from the studio's upstairs windows. To the west loomed the majestic form of Mont Sainte-Victoire, linked to the garden by the road to Le Tholonet.

Ancient pistachio tree similar to one Cézanne painted in the courtyard of the Château Noir.

CÉZANNE'S GARDEN: LES LAUVES

I go to paint the landscape every day, the motifs are beautiful and I thus spend my days better here than elsewhere.

—Letter from Cézanne to his son, written from Les Lauves, his garden and studio, September 1906

OPPOSITE

Cézanne's courtyard at Les Lauves, shaded by a Judas tree, also known as a redbud.

IN NOVEMBER 1901, when Cézanne purchased Les Lauves, he acquired a small one-room peasant's cottage constructed of quarried limestone, with a pantiled roof and a half acre of terraced ground planted as an orchard of olive and fig trees. It was irrigated by a narrow channel that flowed along its western boundary toward Aix-en-Provence, an ancient town founded by the Romans. The property is situated beside a steep road now named the avenue Paul Cézanne but then known as the chemin des Lauves. Its high elevation provides some fine views. Downhill it overlooks the magnificent cathedral spire of Saint-Sauveur, while uphill and to the west the majestic mountain peak of Mont Sainte-Victoire can be seen, its pale limestone escarpments towering high above verdant fields and forest like a volcano's peak. The play of light on the silvery white escarpments of the mountain changes throughout the day, especially in the late afternoon, when its face is illuminated by the fiery colors of a setting sun.

Cézanne cherished the property's ancient olive trees with their gnarled, contorted trunks and gray leaves; he would be dismayed to know that today few of the old trees survive, having been afflicted first by a series of severe winter freezes and then by diseases that killed off the remaining, weakened trees. He acquired the property for reasons similar to those of his friend Renoir, who purchased Les Collettes near Nice to conserve an old olive orchard, where many of the five-hundred-year-old trees still survive.

Like Renoir, Cézanne disliked change.

Both despised the spread of suburbia and industrialization and yearned for earlier times. They were ardent conservationists. Cézanne summed up his dislike of development and industrialization in a letter he wrote to his niece, Paule Conil, in 1902, when he explained his reason for no longer wanting to paint one of his favorite Mediterranean motifs, the town of L'Estaque: "Unfortunately, what we call progress is none other than the invasion of bipeds who never cease until they have finished turning everything into horrible quays with gas towers and—worse still—electrical lighting. What times do we live in!"

He sought an unspoiled Eden, an idealized perception of Valhalla, where the frenetic pace of an increasingly commercialized world could seem far away, and where an eccentric, controversial, visionary painter could live out his final years in peace and contentment, with landscape motifs either within his garden or within an easy walk beyond its fieldstone boundary walls.

Cézanne, having paid a mere two thousand francs for the site, immediately hired an architect known as Mourgues to design and build a house while retaining the existing one-room peasant's cottage as an outbuilding for storage. The resulting new structure, however, displeased him. He had wanted a residence that looked old and spartan, but what the architect produced was a "fantastical villa with a cut-off roof and a wooden balcony, and a paraphernalia of ceramics and varnished wood."

To Emile Bernard, a young friend of Vincent van Gogh, Cézanne complained: "You can't get anything from anyone anymore. I have paid to

OPPOSITE

Olive orchard near Cézanne's garden, bordered with bearded iris, showing how part of the half-acre property probably looked when he first acquired it for a studio. After Cézanne's death a series of prolonged winter freezes and disease weakened many of the trees and caused their decline.

have a place built here, but the architect has refused to carry out my wishes."

What Cézanne had failed to convey to the architect (or the architect ignored in his desire for professional integrity) was that he wanted more of a studio than a home, and a residence that was inoffensive in its rural surroundings. Undaunted, Cézanne had all ostentation removed and the superfluous ornamentation destroyed. Everything that might detract from his painting was banished, and even so he chose never to live there; he would use the residence only as an atelier, a studio. He walked downhill at the end of every day to spend evenings with his wife in an apartment they rented on the rue Boulegon.

Nevertheless, Bernard was impressed with the final result: "The house is an orange ochre, its shape is simple, quite basic. Apart from the slightly meager fireplace, it is of fine taste. . . . The roof has two gables, the cornice is made of three rows of tiles, just as used to be the case for the most exquisite ancient homes of Provence."

What Bernard witnessed a hundred years ago is what visitors to Les Lauves experience to this day—a garden and studio so imbued with the painter that his spirit still seems to be present.

OPPOSITE

Olive orchard near Les Lauves, with Aleppo pines in the background. These olives are growing in red clay soil typical of the area. Cézanne greatly admired olive trees for their silvery foliage and the way their rounded outline and shimmering leaves contrast boldly with the darker foliage of evergreens.

During Cézanne's stewardship of Les Lauves, Europe was experiencing a golden age of horticulture marked by exotic new flowers from Japanese nurseries and by laborsaving devices such as the rotary lawn mower, which allowed homeowners to have neatly trimmed lawns, and the rubber garden hose, which allowed timely watering of flower beds and vast, formal, uniform beds of flowering annuals. But Cézanne's idea of a garden did not envision contrived garden spaces filled with alien plants or such rigid control over nature. He recognized the need for a wall to screen himself and his garden from the outside world; he needed paths to walk around his property, steps to negotiate its slopes, and terraces from which to admire its splendid views. But he wanted a garden as close to nature as possible, short of its becoming a jungle of weeds or a neglected wilderness.

Cézanne found tranquility in his beloved garden and in the countryside immediately beyond its doorstep. Its studio views of the majestic mountain were as much a part of his garden as his cultivated half acre of Eden. Les Lauves became his secluded sanctuary, and its gardener, Vallier, a symbol of the dignity and peace Cézanne discovered there. The artist's last years were happy and productive. At his death, at age sixty-seven, he left a legacy of more than 950 oil paintings and 650 watercolors, and a property that is the most visited museum site in Provence.

Although Cézanne lived only five years after purchasing his walled half acre of land, it served him well, the structure providing him with a spacious indoor studio and the garden excelling

as an outdoor studio. This is where he worked ceaselessly, virtually a recluse, alternating walks around the garden in search of intimate garden motifs with walks in the nearby countryside for wilder or more expansive landscapes. These walks were punctuated by long sessions in his garden studio painting still-life arrangements or painstakingly putting the finishing touches to canvases started *en plein air*. In addition to the orchard of old olive trees and mature fig trees,

within the high stone wall was a grove of tall Aleppo pines that Cézanne painted framing the wall and Mont Sainte-Victoire in the distance. Both *The Big Trees* (1904) and *The Garden at Les Lauves* (1906) show views from inside his studio garden, with the big pines featured in both compositions.

Cézanne especially liked to paint patterns
formed by an outstretched weave of interlocking branches. In his painting entitled *Orchard*
(1890–1895), almost three-quarters of the canvas has the branches of orchard trees as its focus,
the spaces between the network of branches organized into irregular shapes. Though the painting is not of his olive orchard, it features a wall
and orchard trees similar to those at Les Lauves.

On the ground floor of the studio are two
rooms, a bathroom, kitchen, and pantry. The
two larger rooms were designed as bedrooms
but never served that purpose, and today they
function as an administration office and gift
shop.

From the front door a wide staircase leads
directly to the studio, which is immense. To the
south, looking downhill, two large casement
windows open out onto the garden and the
cathedral spire of Aix. To the north a gigantic

window looks out onto a curtain of foliage from
mature trees and shrubs, the thick verdure presenting a rich mosaic of green. In Cézanne's day,
however, he would have been able to see beyond,
to take in a spectacular view of Mont Sainte-
Victoire, now hidden by the burgeoning trees.

The splendid vistas from both the studio
windows and the garden terrace feature in several of Cézanne's paintings of his garden, most
notably *The Garden Terrace at Les Lauves* (1902–
1906). This same painting, rendered in pale watercolors, was probably a preliminary study for a
more finished work he never lived to paint. The
walls of Cézanne's terrace can be seen support-
ing an assortment of potted plants grown by
Vallier. Made of rectangular limestone blocks,
the walls provide a strong geometric framing element for the foreground and a stepped
descent to the strong contrast of foliage in the
middle ground, with the hazy outline of Mont

BELOW

Flight of stone steps leads from the courtyard to the upper garden, with a potted hydrangea resting on the gravel.

FOLLOWING PAGES

The upper garden seen through the large window of Cézanne's upstairs studio, with the trunks and branches of rowan trees adding structural highlights and a rich tapestry of foliage colors.

Sainte-Victoire rising above the screen of foliage. The painting appears to be unfinished, for what looks like a dead tree striking the sky on the right could be a live redbud with a healthy canopy of heart-shaped leaves intended to fill the unfinished portion at the top of the composition, above the mountain.

One can imagine Cézanne on the second floor of his studio, frequently looking out from his high window onto the walled enclosure that represented his secret world, finding inspiration in the venerable olives and figs, with their weathered branches like outstretched arms embracing the sky and the light. Beyond them the pines towered above the wall, framing a magnificent view of the countryside and the majestic form of Mont Sainte-Victoire. The limestone mountain reminded him of a nude reclining woman, her head arching back and her breasts thrust high.

A typical day for Cézanne would be to rise early, at first light, and walk or ride by car to Les Lauves from his apartment in Aix. He would collect his painting paraphernalia from his studio, descend a flight of steps hewn from quarry stones onto his terraced patio, perhaps chat with Vallier about garden chores for the day, and then depart through the entrance gates into the surrounding countryside, where he would paint until noon. Invariably dressed in black, looking for all the world like a dignified undertaker, he would search for dramatic natural motifs: farmhouses framed by avenues of tall trees, country lanes shaded by frowning cliffs and arching branches, garden terraces decorated with ivy and reverting to wilderness. By noon he would return to his studio terrace and continue to paint in the shade—sometimes an intimate watercolor of a potted geranium or of pines in the sheltered corner of his garden, or a study of his gardener seated in front of lush greenery. He painted slowly, mostly in the open, often taking years to complete his works in oils. Even his watercolors were worked on in stages over months and years, yet they give the impression of being executed spontaneously, in an hour or two.

In the late afternoon he might summon his transportation again to return to his landscape motifs in the neighborhood. Eventually the approach of dusk would remind him to return to his studio, take a final stroll through the garden, and then head home to his city apartment for an evening meal and time with his family.

Evergreen English ivy climbs a tree in Cézanne's garden. Cézanne considered ivy-girdled trees a decorative element, adding maturity and character to a landscape.

OPPOSITE

Potted Plants (1888–90); The Barnes Foundation, Merion, Pennsylvania. Vining ivy-leaf geraniums thread their flowering stems through evergreen vinca foliage.

In 1904, two years before Cézanne's death, he invited artist Emile Bernard to Les Lauves, giving him strict instructions to come to the studio on the ground floor and to wait for him there. The young man walked up the road and paused to catch his breath from the steep climb. "Even from afar I could see my old master's studio. It stands out in the landscape, presenting to the sun its peaceful façade, its closed shutters, its flat roof with two gables." He felt Cézanne was there, urging him on. "I started to walk again. I have reached my goal," he wrote.

Bernard entered the high wooden gate and walked through the garden, which sloped down to a narrow canal. The property shimmered with olive trees, and at the bottom, its grove of mature pines stabbed the sky. From under a large stone, he took a key and opened the new and silent house that the sun seemed to bake. In the ground-floor room an easel and paints were there for him to use until Cézanne was ready to take a break from his work. As he began a still life Cézanne had set up for him, he could hear the master working on the floor above. "I could hear him walking to and fro in the top studio; it was like a meditative stroll back and forth in his room; he would also come down, go into the garden, sit down, then rush back up the stairs."

Bernard described how he often saw Cézanne in his garden looking disheartened. He would murmur that something had interrupted his thinking, and he would stare straight ahead at the rooftops of Aix basking in the sunlight, with the cathedral tower striking the sky. "We would discuss atmosphere, color, the Impressionists, and questions that bothered him; the passing

of tones . . ." wrote Bernard. Not only was Cézanne's usual system of painting excruciatingly slow, but he often left a canvas unfinished for years before returning with sufficient confidence to make further progress. He was merciless in destroying anything that did not meet his exacting standards, and even much of his surviving work carries no signature, for he rarely considered a canvas completed. He would sign only his exhibited work, and then mostly in red paint, as though he had sweated blood in its execution.

When he was invited into the upstairs studio, Bernard saw the large room he later described as a pasty gray, absorbing the beaming light from the massive north window. Cézanne was working on a canvas of three skulls on an Oriental rug. On a larger easel was a much bigger canvas of nude women bathing. On the wall of the workshop, beyond landscape canvases that were drying, sat green apples on a plank of wood.

Bernard wanted to ask the master to pose for him but lost his nerve when he realized how valuable time was to his mentor; however, he summoned enough courage to ask for a photograph. Cézanne agreed, and Bernard posed him in front of one of his large *Bathers* canvases.

Cézanne spent every day of his last four years in his studio, in his garden, or on the mountain. In 1905 two art dealers were struck by the apparent chaos of the painter's interiors. After his visit, one wrote: "In all corners lay canvases still stretched on their wooden sub-frames, or rolled up. Some had been left on chairs and been crushed. His studios, the one in the rue Boulegon and that in the country, were in great disorder, simply a mess. The walls were bare, the

OPPOSITE

Corner of Cézanne's upstairs studio, showing an A-frame ladder he used to paint large canvases, such as the Bathers *series, rendered mostly in blue tones.*

light crude. Half-empty tubes, long-dried-up brushes, their silk stiff with color, and remains of meals which became models for still lifes littered the tables. In a corner a whole collection of garden parasols, crudely put together by some shopkeeper in town with metal tips from the local blacksmith, lay next to a collection of hunters' game bags to carry picnics to the country."

The two men observed a large painting of female bathers in progress, in predominantly blue tones, the figures themselves almost life-size. It was one of Cézanne's great series of masterpieces entitled *Les Grandes Baigneuses* (*The Bathers*). This particular study was later purchased by the Barnes Foundation, in Philadelphia. "I hardly dare admit it," commented Cézanne to his visitors. "I've been working at it since 1894. I wanted to paint it in thick oils as Courbet used to."

There was also a more colorful work in progress showing Cézanne's gardener—a superb painting rendered in a mosaic of tile-shaped brushstrokes. "If I do him well, it will mean my theory is correct," he mused. He did not amplify his remarks, but we may guess that he meant that his leaning toward greater abstraction was correct. It was to be his final canvas, and indeed he did it well enough to inspire other great artists, among them Picasso and Braque, to herald the entirely new artistic style known as cubism.

Ironically, the mountain beyond the walls of Cézanne's garden, which provided more subjects for him than any other, and which he considered as much a part of his garden as his olive orchard and stone terraces, was to precipitate his death. He was caught in a severe thunderstorm one afternoon and drenched to the skin while trying to find shelter. Already suffering frail health from diabetes, he stumbled over exposed tree roots as he picked his way downhill and became disoriented by the sheets of blinding rain while thrashing through thickets of scrub oak and holly. Exhausted, he soon collapsed among heaps of rocks and bushes of wild rosemary at the side of the main road. The driver of a laundry cart found him delirious and close to death from exposure. He was loaded onto the cart unconscious and taken home. Though he seemed to recover and tried to complete his landmark portrait of Vallier, he caught pneumonia and died a week later in his Aix apartment, October 22, 1906.

CHAPTER THREE

CÉZANNE'S ARTISTIC LEGACY

It is our business as artists to convey the thrill of nature's permanence along with elements and the appearance of all its changes. . . . So I join together nature's straying hands. . . . From all sides, here, there, and everywhere, I select colors, tones, and shades; I set them down, I bring them together. . . . They make lines. They become objects—rocks, trees—without my thinking about them. They take on volume, value.

—PAUL CÉZANNE, DESCRIBING HIS OEUVRE

Sycamore tree in Cézanne's garden, with bark shining from a shower of rain.

JULIE MANET, NIECE of Edouard Manet, the Impressionist painter, provided a wonderful description of Cézanne: "He looks like a cutthroat, with large red eyeballs standing out from his head in amost ferocious manner, a rather fierce-looking pointed beard, and a way of talking that makes the dishes rattle." The vivid description is as marvelous a portrait of Cézanne as one of his own self-portrait paintings. But as Julie Manet later discovered, far from being a cutthroat, he had the gentlest nature possible. "In spite of a total disregard for the dictionary of manners, he shows a politeness which no other man here would have shown. He is one of the most liberal artists I have ever seen," she concluded.

Cézanne was born illegitimate; the marriage of his parents legitimized him when he was five. His father was an authoritarian, and miserly. A hatter by trade, who eventually took control of the only bank in Aix, he wanted his son to follow him into the banking profession by becoming a financial attorney. But Cézanne disliked office work and showed an early aptitude for art. A serious student, he would spend days in the mountains around Aix, reading Virgil and French classics. Emile Zola, who was to become a great literary figure, was his best friend at school. They explored the rugged countryside together and in summer enjoyed swimming in the crystal-clear streams and rivers that flowed from the nearby mountains.

Cézanne had extremely low self-esteem and lacked social graces. He often ate using only his knife, drained coffee spills from his sau-

cer by raising it to his lips, and was so short-tempered, he earned the nickname *l'écorché* (the man without skin). When he abandoned his banking job and moved to Paris to study art, his strong Provençal accent created the impression of a country bumpkin. This effect was intensified by his habit of wearing paint-stained overalls, even at formal functions, and a well-worn wool cap. He maintained the appearance of a homeless person who had not bathed in weeks.

In the great French capital, Cézanne spent most afternoons at the Louvre sketching the masters. He soon enrolled at the Atelier Suisse art school, where he made the acquaintance of the rebellious circle of painters known as Impressionists, who sought to revolutionize the art world. In particular, he established a friendship with Camille Pissarro, an artist ten years his senior, and then later with the young upstarts Claude Monet and Pierre-Auguste Renoir. Pissarro, born to a Jewish merchant family in the Virgin Islands, was at the height of his Impressionist powers and willing to accept Cézanne as a student. Between 1872 and 1874, Cézanne's world was governed by Pissarro, who had settled near Pontoise, northwest of Paris. The two traveled the countryside together in search of compositions. Pissarro's influence was profound. He forbade the use of black in order to draw Cézanne away from his tendency to paint dark motifs and encouraged him to paint directly from nature. Much of Cézanne's early work—*The Murder* (1867–68) and *The Abduction* (1867), for example—reflects the demons of his flawed personality and his aberrant behavior. He was a tortured soul, demoralized by his father, torn between

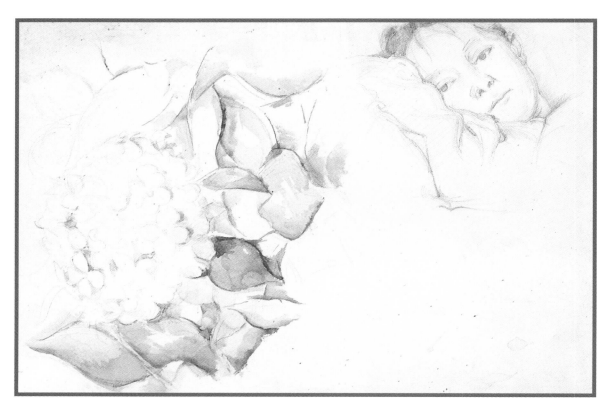

Paul *Cézanne,* Madame Cézanne (Hortense Fiquet) with Hydrangeas; *private collection. A tender rendering of Cézanne's wife, looking sleepy-eyed in bed. Her name, Hortense, means "hydrangea" in French, explaining the significance of the flowers.*

the disciplined and the undisciplined, man and nature, civilization and the wilderness. Taking offense easily, Cézanne treated every new human encounter with suspicion. He retreated hastily from gatherings of friends, was painfully shy among women, and could easily be reduced to tears by a compliment; he once knelt before Rodin, thanking him profusely for praising his work. He disliked intimacy and could not bear to be touched, even with a handshake. In spite of his discomfort among women, in 1869 Cézanne began an affair with a young model named Hortense Fiquet. She was eighteen and he was thirty; in 1872 they had a son while he was living in Paris. Cézanne hid the liaison from his father

for fear of losing his financial support and chose to marry Hortense only a few months before his father's death.

Yet Cézanne's work is full of sexual innuendo, some of it tender and romantic, as in his painting *Madame Cézanne (Hortense Fiquet) with Hydrangeas* (1885), and some of it highly erotic, as in *Modern Olympia* (1873), which depicts a dapper Cézanne seated in shadow, admiring the charms of a voluptuous nude courtesan flooded in light. Cézanne also produced what is possibly the most sacrilegious, most licentious image ever painted—*Lot's Daughters* (1861), which shows the biblical father conducting incest with one daughter in the presence of the other.

Under Pissarro's influence, Cézanne briefly embraced Impressionism, the style of artistic expression that sought to convey more than just realistic representations of the world. Using flickering, comma-shaped brushstrokes, the Impressionists captured sensations of light, so their paintings produced brilliantly colorful fleeting auras and a sometimes dreamlike quality that expressed the artist's inner voice. Because the artistic merit of a painting was at the time judged by its realism, Impressionism was at first ridiculed as childish and unprofessional. Three major influences spurred Impressionism: the flow into Europe of Japanese art with its animated style and intimate motifs; the invention of oil paints in tubes, which allowed artists more freedom to paint directly from nature; and the invention of the snapshot camera, which captured images more realistically than any artist could paint, encouraging progressive painters to forsake realism and become more expressive in their work, to the point of exaggeration.

The ten leading proponents of Impressionism at the time of Cézanne's conversion, including Pissarro, were seven other men—Claude Monet, Pierre-Auguste Renoir, Alfred Sisley, Gustave Caillebotte, Frédéric Bazille, Edgar Degas, and Edouard Manet—and two women, Mary Cassatt (an American heiress) and Berthe Morisot (a Parisienne). Other famous painters of the day who are considered post-Impressionists include Gauguin and van Gogh. Gauguin also studied under Pissarro, and Cézanne hated him, claiming that Gauguin tried to steal his thunder by copying his style.

Finding Paris a difficult place to work,

Cézanne would leave the capital for long periods to live at the Jas de Bouffan, enjoying its parklike woodland, farmland, and ponds. Although his father despised Cézanne's choice of career, he gave his son room for a studio in the attic. Art historians believe that because of his father's financial support, Cézanne was able to be more liberal in his artistic expression than others of the day. An important influence on his artistic yearnings were the works of Eugène Delacroix and Gustave Courbet: Delacroix for his heroic themes of combat and a bravura style of painting, and Courbet for his moody landscapes and shocking images of young women in sexually provocative poses.

Though Impressionism was at first ridiculed by the Parisian art establishment, eventually it won public acclaim and changed the way the world perceives art. Monet and Renoir's more romantic style of painting was easier to appreciate than Cézanne's, and so it took longer for Cézanne's work to gain acclaim. Cézanne was finally recognized as a leading artist of his day in 1895—at age fifty-six—when he achieved the success of a one-man show in Paris.

Monet and Renoir were friends from their student years; they not only roomed together but traveled together on painting trips, challenging each other, and helped each other financially during difficult years. Both held Cézanne in the highest regard among contemporary painters. Although he was only a year older, they looked on him as a sage and defended his art against ridicule. Both acquired important art collections that included works by Cézanne, as did Caillebotte, Gauguin, Degas, and Paul Signac. Monet eventually acquired eleven Cézanne paintings for his collection of Impressionist art.

Dr. Paul Gachet, who treated Cézanne, Pissarro, Renoir, and van Gogh for psychological problems, also owned Cézanne's work. In later years, when Henri Matisse and Pablo Picasso recognized the greatness of Cézanne, Matisse

The reflections of Monet's famous water garden, at Giverny, became the artist's favorite motif in his old age. Cézanne visited Monet often, staying at the nearby Hôtel Baudy. He greatly admired Monet as a painter but probably considered the garden too contrived and labor-intensive for his own liking.

bought one of Cézanne's *Bathers,* and Picasso reported one day to his dealer that he had bought Cézanne's Mont Sainte-Victoire: "Not the painting—the mountain!" Indeed, Picasso purchased the Château de Vauvenargues on the side of the mountain, with land that included part of the landscape Cézanne loved to paint. Picasso declared that Cézanne was "my one and only master."

Even the great British sculptor Sir Henry Moore was influenced by Cézanne's work. His

cherished acquisition was a painting in the *Bathers* series entitled *Three Bathers* (1875), which shows three playful Rubenesque nude women on a riverbank, with strong, rounded forms, one noticeably pregnant. In an interview Moore explained his reason for acquiring the painting, and how it inspired him to do a set of plaster sculptures entitled *Three Bathers, after Cézanne* (1978):

"Perhaps another reason why I fell for it is that the type of woman he portrays is the same kind I like. Each of the figures I could turn into a piece of sculpture, very simply. . . . Not young girls but that wide, broad, mature woman. Look at the back view of the figure on the left. What a strength . . . almost like the back of a gorilla, that kind of flatness. But it has also this, this romantic idea of women. [Three] lots of long tresses, and the hair he has given them."

Monet, Renoir, and Cézanne were astute observers of nature, and toward the end of their lives each established an idyllic garden—their perception of Eden—which became the focus of their art. Monet established his garden at Giverny, an hour's train ride north of Paris, where his water lily pond was his favorite motif. Pissarro also had a beautiful garden combining flowers and vegetables, which he painted in his later years, though it no longer survives.

Renoir's garden retreat was Les Collettes, his farm and olive orchard near Nice. Despite the fact that Impressionism bound Monet, Renoir, and Cézanne by a common thread, and the gardens they established inspired masterpieces, the properties are as different from each other as their painting techniques. Collectively, however, they embodied the elements that would define the appeal of Impressionism.

When Cézanne finally bought his half acre of ground on which to build a studio and cultivate a garden, he sought not to produce a colorful, labor-intensive garden full of shimmering flower petals and carefully orchestrated color harmonies as did his friend Claude Monet. His garden was filled with the more enduring images he discovered in nature—the organic structural silhouettes of branches, vines, and tree trunks; the billowing, vibrating screens of foliage; the solidity of fieldstone walls, limestone blocks, and stone terraces.

COMPARISON WITH MONET'S AND RENOIR'S GARDENS

When people today are asked to name a great French Impressionist artist, three names come readily to mind—Monet for his shimmering water lily paintings, Renoir for his sensuous nude women with rosy skin tones, and Cézanne for his vibrating landscapes. Though Cézanne admired the work of Monet and Renoir, he dismissed van Gogh's art as the work of a madman and Gauguin's as plagiarizing his own. Manet called Cézanne's paintings "foul," and even Cézanne's boyhood friend Zola had such a poor opinion of his work that he satirized him in his popular novel *L'Oeuvre (The Work)*. It told the tragic story of a frustrated artist who never gained recognition and who eventually hanged himself. The book angered Cézanne and ended their friendship.

Monet, Renoir, and Cézanne all achieved artistic acclaim in their lifetimes after years of rejection by the Paris Salon and vitriolic ridicule

by the Paris press. After they became financially independent, each developed a beautiful garden—Monet at Giverny, northwest of Paris; Renoir at Cagnes-sur-Mer, west of Nice; and Cézanne at Aix-en-Provence in the shadow of Mont Sainte-Victoire. Remarkably, all three gardens have survived more than a hundred years of turbulent events, have been restored mostly by American funding, and are now thronged by tens of thousands of visitors a year.

A visit to each garden reveals completely different design philosophies. Monet's garden, at Giverny in the Normandy countryside, is

Renoir's garden, Les Collettes, is located near Nice and more closely resembles Cézanne's garden than any other among the Impressionists. Featuring an orchard of five-hundred-year-old olive trees, Renoir bought the property to save the ancient trees from development. He maintained it in as natural condition as possible, except for a rose garden cultivated by his wife below the main house.

43

essentially a flower garden, though it has two parts. First is the Clos Normand, which Monet began as a means to have flowers for arrangements to paint when the weather was bad. He orchestrated several dominant color harmonies, especially red, pink, and green; blue and yellow; and yellow, orange, and red. He then established a water garden, the focus of which is a collection of water lilies floating on the surface of a pond.

Both the Clos Normand and the water garden yielded a vast number of paintings, and in his later years the water lily pond, with its exquisite reflections, became his entire focus.

Monet described his five-acre garden as his greatest work of art, and garden historians have identified more than a hundred special planting designs that made it unique. Monet created the most beautiful and the most innovative private garden in all of Europe.

His flower garden, for example, features a *grand allée*—a broad gravel path leading from the house to the bottom of the garden. It is arched over by six metal supports covered in climbing roses. The path is bordered with perennials, and annual nasturtiums creep in from the sides to make a floral tunnel.

Much of the inspiration for Monet's water garden comes from his study of Japanese landscape design. The Japanese influence is evident in his arched "moon-viewing" bridge, curtains of bamboo, and a stroll path that completely encircles the pond. The water garden is a space for introspection, with viewing places along the path to encourage visitors to look inward at the pond reflections and its islands of water lilies.

Renoir's garden, at Cagnes-sur-Mer, near Nice, is essentially an ancient olive grove surrounding a sunny wildflower meadow and a rose garden. Renoir loved roses because their flowers had substance and their petals contained the flesh tones of the women and children he loved to paint; he considered the old olive orchard spangled with wildflowers a good place to pose his voluptuous nudes. The model was generally seated beneath the trees, while he was comfortably seated inside a studio with glass walls to avoid sunburn or chills.

Les Lauves is closer in design philosophy to Les Collettes than to Giverny. Both Renoir's and Cézanne's gardens featured an orchard of olive trees, a steeply sloping site, and a high elevation offering views over a surrounding valley, but Renoir's also featured a lot of flowers, while Cézanne's relied more on foliage and structure for interest.

Monet and Renoir first visited Cézanne while on a trip through the south of France, seeking motifs along the Mediterranean coastline. He was still living at the Jas de Bouffan. In turn Cézanne often visited Monet at Giverny and Renoir at the nearby village of La Roche-Guyon, where both he and Renoir rented summer homes. Renoir recounted fond memories of painting the countryside near Aix with Cézanne. When he learned that Cézanne felt uncomfortable using a live model, he encouraged Cézanne to watch him paint nudes.

CHAPTER FOUR

A VISIT TO CÉZANNE'S GARDEN TODAY

A wonderful visit!

—MARILYN MONROE'S ENTRY IN THE VISITOR'S BOOK,
AFTER VISITING CÉZANNE'S STUDIO AND GARDEN, 1955

OPPOSITE

View along the bottom of Cézanne's garden, showing a
retaining wall on the right that drops steeply to neighboring
gardens. The plant with contorted branches is a late-leafing
fig, probably a surviving tree from the time the property
was an orchard of fig and olive trees.

ODAY WE CAN NOT only explore Cézanne's garden and visit his second-floor studio, we can follow in his footsteps to the very foothills of Mont Sainte-Victoire and see the inspiration for his art and his garden aesthetic. Like many visitors, I experienced a revelation the moment I stepped into Cézanne's garden. I felt I was stepping into one of his canvases, for immediately I was aware of the extraordinary diversity of greens and the way solid, hard-edged structural accents—walls, terraces, limestone blocks, and the house façade—were veiled with the expressive branches of trees and vines.

The garden is evidence that Cézanne's powerful painting technique was heavily influenced by its setting. The views and colors, the structures and textures, the shimmering vibrations in the atmosphere all still exist there in his garden and the surrounding countryside. It simply took an astute person—one completely in harmony with nature—to recognize their force and form, and to make a garden as he wanted to paint it, as expressive in its individuality as his painting technique. The bones Cézanne laid have since filled in to create a mature garden with the same brooding atmosphere and natural forms he cherished at the Jas de Bouffan and coveted at the Château Noir.

Cézanne's life was full of contradictions, and the garden that survives him at Les Lauves is no exception. The garden that Cézanne knew, the one he created and painted, and the garden that survives today, nearly one hundred years since his death, in 1906, are understandably different. Yet the more mature garden that survives him is still a reflection of his art, a living testimony to the enduring elements of nature that he cherished, and faithful to his oeuvre. Increasing numbers of visitors each year crowd into his upstairs studio, then spill out onto his courtyard and filter into the garden along a labyrinth of bowery paths.

The garden today no longer includes an orchard. It is full of trees and billowing shrubs that have matured along meandering paths to fill the garden with a verdure Cézanne would have admired. Many are native trees (like redbuds and the Aleppo pines) that sprouted spontaneously on the site, or shrublike ornamental woody

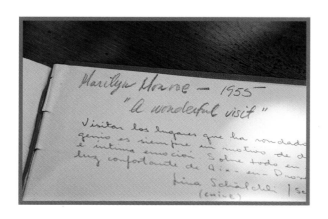

LEFT

Marilyn Monroe's signature in the guest book at Les Lauves. She visited the property shortly after it opened to the public, in 1955, while she was attending a film festival in nearby St.-Tropez.

RIGHT

Plan of Cézanne's Garden. Cézanne's half-acre restored garden showing the studio, cottage, and courtyard surrounded by a labyrinth of woodland paths that form a series of leaf tunnels leading to clearings. Also marked are the stone terraces, steps, site of the tree house, and the contemporary bamboo tunnel.

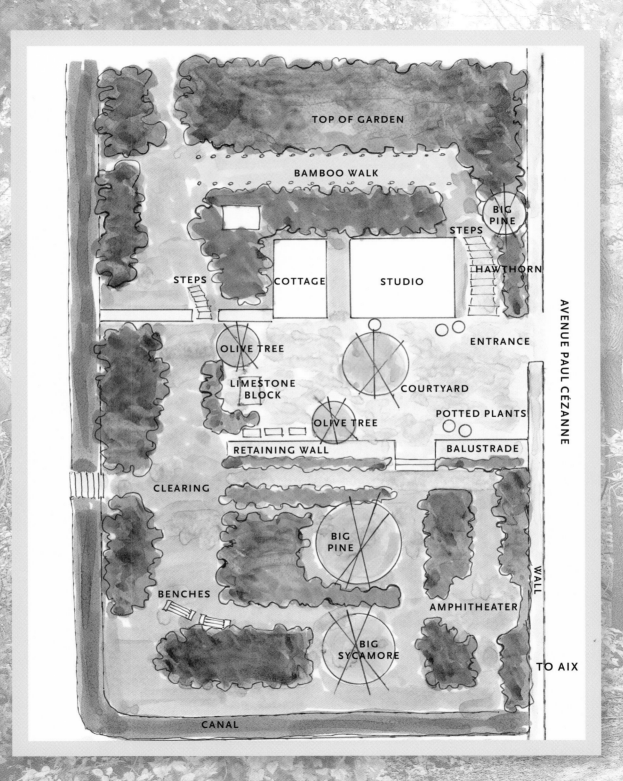

TOP OF GARDEN

BAMBOO WALK

BIG PINE

STEPS

HAWTHORN

STEPS

COTTAGE STUDIO

ENTRANCE

OLIVE TREE

LIMESTONE BLOCK

COURTYARD

OLIVE TREE

POTTED PLANTS

RETAINING WALL

BALUSTRADE

CLEARING

BIG PINE

BENCHES

AMPHITHEATER

BIG SYCAMORE

CANAL

AVENUE PAUL CÉZANNE

WALL

TO AIX

plants (like mock orange and rosemary) that replaced the old olives and figs after disease and a period of heavy frosts killed off most of them. In Cézanne's day the garden was largely a sun-drenched orchard of great charm and character—the olives with tortuous trunks and gnarled branches, their silvery leaves shimmering in the slightest breeze. The mature, fruiting fig trees—planted between the olives—had similarly snaking branches but large, leathery, transluscent leaves that shone like Chinese lanterns when backlit by the sun. In bold contrast, at the bottom of the half-acre property the handsome grove of tall pines—striking the sky with pencil-straight trunks and topknots of dark green needles—provided cool shade for a section of the stony site.

The pines survive, today encircled by plantings of shrubs that replaced the olives and the figs, though there are scattered remnants of these still in the garden.

The steps from Cézanne's studio lead out onto a terraced gravel courtyard. The foundation plants around the front door resemble those Cézanne painted while in residence. The sensation of nature reclaiming the site is carefully orchestrated. Though shrub rosemary and an ancient fruiting fig scramble up the walls on either side of the front door, threatening to invade the house and tear it apart, their tangle of wayward branches is pruned just sufficiently to keep the vines in check. Foliage contrasts abound, such as the slender yellow-green leaf blades of a sedge grass erupting from a tall terra-cotta urn above a planting of bear's breeches (*Acanthus mollis*) displaying lustrous dark green leaves. Many visitors mistake the garden for an untamed wilderness or a garden in decline, but in reality it strikes exactly the right note of nature's abundance and the frailty of human presence.

LEFT

Along the studio foundation, leaf blades of fountain grass erupt from a terra-cotta olive jar, the naturalistic container planting framed by the contorted branches of a fruiting fig.

OPPOSITE

Entrance to Cézanne's studio, showing a fruiting fig threatening to obliterate the doorway. This effect is not an example of neglect, but a deliberate attempt by the administration to maintain Cézanne's liking for nature's preeminence over man's intrusion.

From the studio windows facing the cathedral in Aix, the high elevation still provides in spring a splendid view of the cathedral spire over an uplifting tapestry of tree colors and shapes. The positioning of these large trees is not accidental. Each is carefully placed so that the pale blue of the olive trees, the porcelain-white flower clusters of the chestnuts, the mint greens of the redbuds, and the black-greens of the pines present a rich play of billowing color, texture, and form.

Emerging from the cool, subdued light of the studio into the bright sunlight of the courtyard, the visitor is lured deeper into the garden by dark cavernous openings in the curtains of foliage and rough-hewn steps leading down from the terrace into the heart of a woodland.

The paths through the woodland sometimes run straight as an arrow, completely covered with a canopy of leaves, their dappled shadows making patterns like those seen in many of Cézanne's paintings of woodland. At points where the paths intersect, the canopy is thinned to create a sunlit glade. There are twists and turns, but everywhere along the path the trunks of trees and the multiple stems of tall shrubs are limbed high by pruning. Instead of a haphazard tangle of interlocking branches, there is a beautiful tracery of branch silhouettes to frame distant oases of sunlight.

BELOW

Cézanne brought in from the countryside rough fieldstones and quarry stones to build terraces and steps, allowing ivy to soften the hard lines of the stone. Though parts of Cézanne's garden, like this, resemble a garden in decline, the impression is deliberate.

OPPOSITE

Patterns and contrasts of sunlight and shadow are favorite components of Cézanne's garden and landscape paintings. This sunlit glade is at the heart of Cézanne's woodland garden.

OPPOSITE

View of Cézanne's woodland garden from the studio's front entrance, looking out across the gravel courtyard. A remnant of an old olive tree exhibits silvery foliage, with autumn tints evident in the leaves of redbuds and other deciduous trees.

TOP RIGHT

Cushions of sedge grass contrast with the leathery, indented leaves of English ivy along a path in Cézanne's woodland garden.

BOTTOM RIGHT

Mature sycamore in Cézanne's garden, mantled with English ivy, and echoing the sycamores at the Jas de Bouffan (page 12).

Many of the paths are paved with broken flat stones, and at intervals during the blooming season their gray is enlivened with a carpeting effect from the spent pink petals of redbud trees and white-petaled mock orange blossoms.

There are flowers along the paths wherever sufficient light penetrates the leaf canopy, but these are usually mere pinpricks of color, mostly from yellow buttercups, pink jupiter's beard (*Centranthus ruber*), and white wild onion indigenous to the site.

A mass planting of jupiter's beard stretches like a broad brushstroke along the bottom boundary of the garden, its slender flower stems holding aloft myriad airy flower panicles. These perennial plants do not obscure the trees beyond but produce a veiling effect—the same veiling sensation seen in many of Cézanne's landscape paintings.

English ivy is everywhere, used as a ground cover along shady slopes, vining up into trees, and softening the studio's expanse of stucco. Moreover, the spicy herbal fragrances of rosemary, thyme, and scented-leaf geraniums combine with the resinous aroma of the pine needles, pervading the atmosphere with the scent of the fields that Cézanne adored.

The current administration—with the aid of director Michel Fraisset and staff interpreter Catherine Cazin—makes a conscious effort to maintain the garden in the spirit of Cézanne. Not only have they established a design philosophy for the garden, but they also strive to introduce elements from Cézanne's paintings to create a garden of artistic merit.

In the quest to maintain Cézanne's woodland garden as a garden rather than an untamed wilderness, the administration specifically seeks to establish five levels of interest: the ground floor, planted with ground-cover plants for weed control (such as English ivy and vinca); the herbaceous level, using woodland wildflowers up to knee level (such as wood anemones and forget-me-nots); the shrub level, comprising mostly woody plants that reach head height (such as mock orange and kerria); the main understory, using small trees (like redbuds and chain trees); and the tree canopy itself, using tall, spreading trees like chestnuts, sycamore, and Aleppo pines.

These woodland layers are not always obvious, since the forces of change and renewal result in a constant intermingling and blurring of the edges between each layer.

The garden was relatively young when Cézanne died, so what remains has reached a maturity that Cézanne never lived to see but that he undoubtedly hoped to achieve. Considering his fondness for the structural and verdant beauty of trees and shrubs and the complexities of the color green, the garden is as much a statement of Cézanne's art as Giverny is of Monet's and Les Collettes is of Renoir's.

RIGHT
High-elevation view from the parking area for Cézanne's garden, with billowing chestnut trees heavily laden with blossom in the foreground. Spires of dark green juniper frame the rooftops of Aix-en-Provence.

After Cézanne's death and burial in the Saint-Sauveur churchyard, the studio remained closed for fifteen years. In 1921 it was bought from the artist's son, Paul Cézanne Jr., by poet Marcel Joannon, who lived there until the end of his life, writing under the pseudonym Marcel Provence. A Cézanne bibliophile, Joannon published numerous articles about the artist and gathered thousands of clippings about Cézanne from all over the world, many of which are pub-

View along one of Cézanne's woodland paths, from the courtyard. The garden descends a slope by a series of terraces.

lished in a booklet entitled *L'année Cézanienne* (The Year of Cézanne) in 1933, revised 1935.

Joannon used only the ground floor of the house as living quarters and left the upstairs studio untouched. By leaving the studio alone, he felt he was "preserving a precious inheritance, a spiritual wealth encased in the walls and the garden."

Joannon left no will, and with intensive de-

velopment creeping up the hill, his death might well have jeopardized the survival of the property. Fortunately, art historian John Rewald and art patron James Lord recognized the value of this important link to Cézanne. In 1952 they jointly saved the property from destruction by forming the Cézanne Memorial Committee to solicit funds for its preservation. With funds from 114 American art patrons (including Erich Maria Remarque, author of *All Quiet on the Western Front*), as well as philanthropists around Aix-en-Provence, the property was purchased to serve as a museum.

Entrusted to the University of Aix Marseille, the Atelier Cézanne was opened to the public on July 8, 1954; and one of its earliest visitors was American film actress Marilyn Monroe. Enriched by further financial gifts from Rewald, the studio was transferred to the city of Aix in 1969 and has since become the responsibility of the local department of tourism.

The four central design elements in Cézanne's art are color, structure, texture, and location. They are the same elements Cézanne sought to introduce into his garden when he purchased the property, and they are all present in the garden today in a state of maturity that would no doubt have pleased him. Here today are the "curtains of color" (*les murs verts*) seen in his paintings, the "leaf tunnels" of his paintings (trees and shrubs trimmed of lower branches to make a high leafy canopy like the vaulted ceiling of a cathedral), the chunky limestone blocks he brought in from local quarries to add structural solidity and strength and also to serve as pedestals for container plants. Everywhere along the shady paths today are bold contrasts of leaf form and texture and the accentuated lines of tree trunks.

When Cézanne occupied the property, it had a more open aspect, the house visible on the hillside from a long distance. Today it is entirely concealed by a high stone wall and a thick screen of trees, including billowing chestnuts, arching redbuds, and towering figs. The entrance gate is difficult to find even with directions, for a sign on the street (now paved and renamed avenue Paul Cézanne) is often obscured by ivy. A granite block on an entrance pillar, engraved with the name Cézanne, is also weatherworn and hard to see. There is no room for parking on the busy street; in order to park safely, it is necessary to proceed to the top of the hill, turn right into a housing development, and park in a confined lot shared with residents of a tall, dilapidated apartment building. Even finding the avenue Paul Cézanne can be frustrating. From the one-way ring road system around the center of Aix it is best to follow signs to the Hôpital Regionnaire on the avenue Pasteur; after making the turn, take an immediate right around the hospital buildings. A sign marked ATELIER CÉZANNE then suddenly appears showing a sharp turn, uphill to the right.

Once you have parked, care must be taken to descend a steep public stairway back onto the avenue Paul Cézanne, and since the pavement is narrow, visitors must literally hug the wall with elbows tucked in so that quarry trucks, tour buses, and fast cars can drive by. A puce-colored double-hinged carriage door announces the entrance to Cézanne's studio. The door creaks slowly open. Stepping inside feels like entering

Row of limestone quarry stones, brought into Cézanne's garden to produce terraces and blocky stone contrasts with the softer, flowing lines of multistemmed mock orange and redbud trees, like the building blocks of the Château Noir (see page 14).

the gates of paradise, for there is an over-whelming sense of peace and tranquility. The visitor sees a wide terrace of beige gravel shaded by the arching branches of ivy-girdled trees. A flight of stone steps leads up to the elevated front door, itself almost hidden by vegetation from foundation plantings.

Following a visit to Cézanne shortly after he had moved in, Parisian art dealer Georges Rivier described the same scene visitors see to-day: "The house had no furniture or ornament, it was full of the painter's presence. It only exists because of its complete and obvious harmony with the painter. Nothing there could distract the painter's mind from his concern. Everything that might spark off his meditation was to be found there: materials with shimmering shades of color as well as simple badly painted replicas of such works of art the painter liked or found amusing. Moreover, silence was all-pervasive around the dwelling place."

The studio appears just as Cézanne left it when he died, in 1906. A vertical slot in the north wall of the large upstairs studio room enabled the artist to move out his largest canvases, such as *The Bathers* (1905). The ceiling is twenty feet high, the walls are painted a neutral gray, and the immense picture window on the north wall floods the studio with light even on an overcast day. A long board along the west wall serves as a shelf. The room also contains a plain wooden table, a chest of drawers, a tall A-frame stepladder, a high easel, and a potbellied stove with a long metal stove-pipe poking through the ceiling. Scattered about are a sofa and some chairs with raffia seats similar to ones van Gogh painted in nearby Arles during

a visit from Gauguin. Myriad objects are recog-nizable as motifs in his still-life arrangements—a pyramid of human skulls, a conch shell with pink lips and obvious sexual connotations, a small plaster cupid, the black clock from his painting of the same name, vases, and various items of lo-cal earthenware, as well as step stools, draperies, figurines, and empty bottles. Several dark coats and hats that the artist owned hang in a corner, along with a walking cane and an umbrella. A small crucifix high on the west wall gives a hint of the master's strong religious beliefs. A devout Catholic, he attended mass every Sunday.

Dotted about the walls are a few framed prints indicating Cézanne's personal taste in art: a painting, *La Curée,* by Courbet, Delacroix's *Lion Devouring a Goat* and *Death of Sardanapalus,* and Daumier's *Around the Artist's Studio.* Although Cézanne's studio seems sparse and forbidding, its contents dwarfed by the room's spaciousness, there is gemlike color in the details. Pleasant fragrances evoke a sense of the country and create the aura of a hallowed place conducive to creative inspiration. The mood perfectly matches a description by journalist Leo Lar-guier in an article entitled "Sunday with Paul Cézanne": "Right in the middle of the studio, on a little table, there was a large bouquet of artificial flowers in a vase. In every corner of the room lay fruit, drying or moldy, that was being used for his still lifes, and his studio reeked of country bedrooms where, in autumn, pears and mushrooms might be kept."

What Larguier failed to mention was that Cézanne sometimes used artificial flowers for his floral paintings because he painted so slowly that fresh flowers would die before he could finish the work, but he used fresh fruit like apples and pears since they did not perish as quickly and the colors would remain sharp to the finish. "Apples like to have their portraits painted," Cézanne told an admirer. "They come to you in all their varied scents, speaking to you of the fields they left, the rain that nourished them."

During my own first visit, in autumn 1990, bunches of dried dill provided a smell of the fields, and the aroma of fresh fruits and vegetables pervaded the air, including sprouted onions, ripe oranges, pink peaches, plump yellow-green pears, and a vast variety of apples with green, red, russet, and blushing orange skins.

The studio room is so somber, the fruits are like beacons of light; the intensity of their hues is astonishing against the dark tones of the room. After viewing the studio room and visiting the gift shop filled with Cézanne posters and books, I jostled past incoming crowds and stepped out onto the wide balustraded terrace to begin a stroll through the garden. There were no direction signs indicating where to start, just a choice of paths leading off into tunnels of greenery. Entering the garden is like being lost in a maze or, more accurately, the dark catacombs beneath Paris, the paths are so shadowy and winding and overhung with greenery. A curving flight of steps leads uphill behind the house; more rustic steps of rough-hewn limestone lead down to the bottom of the garden, its boundary marked by an irrigation canal crossed by a rustic bridge.

BELOW LEFT

Flight of rough stone steps descends into Cézanne's shadowy woodland garden from the sunlit courtyard.

BELOW RIGHT

Temporary rustic bridge crosses a canal that marks the western boundary of Cézanne's garden, used by the gardener as a shortcut into the garden.

What visitors see today when they enter the walled property of Les Lauves is more verdure than in Cézanne's day. The shady terrace, paved in pea gravel, is now almost completely canopied with the arching branches of trees. The lime green of a redbud canopy mingles its transluscent foliage with the flashing leaves of an olive, and towering above all are an immense sycamore with marbled bark, and a billowing horse chestnut that produces an avalanche of white cone-shaped flower clusters in early summer. One's entire field of vision is infused with shades of green, while at every turn a weave of strong branch silhouettes etches the scene with structural interest.

At the far end of the terrace a flight of steps leads to a pair of raised decks clustered with tables and chairs. The decks are connected by a flat, narrow bridge and elevated high into the tree canopy so that the structure resembles a Swiss Family Robinson tree house. The decks provide a bird's-eye view of the lower garden, and they are decorated with container plantings. During my visit in early spring these included marguerite daisies and calendulas, yellow roses and purple heliotrope, and also combinations of food crops, such as lettuce and strawberries, peppers and tomatoes.

The decks were not part of Cézanne's original garden. In recent years the administration has begun to invite landscape architects to design temporary theme areas inspired by Cézanne's art, and the rustic decks were the result of this initiative. These themes may change from year to year. On another visit I admired a woodland path embellished along its entire length with vertical bamboo posts painted crimson—a reminder that Impressionist art was influenced by Japan, though Cézanne's art showed the least influence among Impressionist painters.

The principal function of Cézanne's gardener was to prune and fertilize the orchard and to maintain plantings close to the house, especially the large collection of potted plants and vines set around the house foundation. Remarkably, the garden has survived and matured, mostly by the hand of nature, in a way that is a reflection of Cézanne's art. From nature's chaos, a succession of gardeners has tamed the wilderness and produced a half acre of beauty that Cézanne would have admired.

Cézanne's desire for a garden that harmonizes with nature has been fully realized.

LEFT

This rustic tree house in the upper garden at Les Lauves is a temporary design feature erected as a tribute to Cézanne's acute observations of nature and keen interest in conservation.

OPPOSITE

One of two decks that form the temporary tree house, with simple table and chair, and containers filled with decorative plants. Even an old baggage trunk is used as a planter.

CHAPTER FIVE

COLOR, STRUCTURE, TEXTURE, AND THE MACABRE

However does he do it? The moment he dabs two touches of paint on a canvas, the result is brilliant.

—RENOIR, SPEAKING OF CÉZANNE'S ART

Tapestry garden, using mostly the foliage of trees and shrubs to "paint" the landscape, at the Garden House, Buckland Monochoram, in the English countryside.

VISIT A CÉZANNE exhibit and the greens are astounding. Tour Cézanne's garden, or wander into the countryside at the foot of Mont Sainte-Victoire, and there spread before you are the greens of his landscapes—a tapestry composed of patchwork fields of corn, groves of lime-green lindens, forests of dark green junipers. You will see the matte greens of vineyards, the grass greens of winter wheat, the silvery greens of olive groves, the shimmering mint greens of chestnut trees, sycamores, and redbuds—and above all, the billowing black-greens of towering pine trees. Then there is the incredibly blue sky and the unusual red-ochre clay of its plowed fields, together creating one of nature's most pleasing triad color harmonies—blue, orange, and green. Moreover, the vistas that unfold as you walk the paths of Cézanne's garden today or travel the roads skirting his cherished mountain are not only recognizable as Cézanne's motifs, but his paintings seem to capture even the vibrations of a land swept by wind, baked by the sun, quenched by rainfall, nourished by mineral-rich soils, and made friable by cartloads of farmyard manure. In his paintings you also sense the humid atmosphere of a hot day, feel the liquidity of a shaded pool, and almost hear the ubiquitous sound of Provence—the chirping of cicadas.

Many of Paul Cézanne's landscape paintings of woodland and gardens create the impression of a verdant wall of color or a tapestry effect. When one compares *Bend in the Forest Road* (1902–1906) with *The Garden at Les Lauves* (1906), the relatively

Beautiful example of a leaf tunnel, in autumn, similar to the leafy tunnels of trees and shrubs that are a popular Cézanne motif.

OPPOSITE

Paul Cézanne, Bend in the Forest Road; private collection. This is a good example of Cézanne's liking for leaf tunnels and avenues of trees as a subject to paint.

simple scenes of a gravel road curving through woodland and a wall of Cézanne's garden are similar in composition but quite different in execution. Each is composed of a mosaic of brushstrokes representing curtains of color, producing a rich abstract effect. But while *Bend in the Forest Road* is a traditional Cézanne landscape showing a leafy tunnel of trees, with the brushstrokes carefully applied over a period of four years, *The Garden at Les Lauves* appears to have been painted quickly. Showing a portion of Cézanne's garden wall, the flat formality of the wall and a patch of lawn contrasts with a wild, burgeoning landscape beyond. Broad brushstrokes that are vertical, diagonal, horizontal, and semi-circular appear to have been applied more vigorously and more spontaneously than in his earlier work, as though Cézanne had finally mastered the complexity of his technique and condensed into minutes what might have previously taken him years to accomplish.

The power of *The Garden at Les Lauves* inspired art collector Duncan Phillips to explain his reason for purchasing it: "The classicist became at the close of his career as he had been at the beginning, an expressionist. What was expressed was not only his technique but his obsessive conception, his passionate aim to realize with pigments the vitality and organic unity he sensed in nature."

TAPESTRY GARDEN

On my most recent visit to Cézanne's Garden, I discussed with curator Michel Fraisset the idea of adding a vertical or tapestry garden, perhaps in front of Cézanne's studio window, which looks up into a tangle of interweaving trees and shrubs. The space beyond Cézanne's studio window is perfect for a vertical garden because it slopes steeply, and the plants could be positioned so that the window view is filled with beautiful foliage effects, orchestrated to resemble a Cézanne landscape or tapestry.

Vertical gardens (*murs végétaux*) are a dynamic feature of many new French gardens—especially in and around Paris, where confined spaces such as courtyards can have limited ground space but plenty of wall space. Two spectacular examples can be seen today at the Hotel Pershing Hall, off the Champs-Élysées in Paris, along a sunlit wall of a courtyard; and the Parc de Crécy, in Paris, against a high terrace wall. In the Hotel Persh-

ing Hall design the curtain of greenery provides a soothing contrast to the rectangular structure of the building. At the Parc de Crécy, a red angular slash provides a modernistic touch and a similar, but more subdued, contrast.

In small-space city gardens, it makes good sense to take foliage interest high into the sky, since the sight of monotonous expanses of bare wall can be oppressive. There are two favored ways to accomplish a vertical garden. In one the plants are not even rooted in soil but gain anchorage by probing an absorbent felt liner one half inch or more thick. An impervious PVC sheet placed between the absorbent liner and the wall protects the wall from erosion by invasive roots. A nutrient solution dripping down through the felt can provide plant roots with moisture and food, as in a hydroponic system. The water and nutrients are recirculated to create a constantly moist vertical blanket, resulting in lush, luxuriant growth.

When a vertical liner is used to make a vertical garden, pockets must be cut in the felt to accommodate seeds or plants. The plants soon establish a web of roots that mesh together to give strength to the felt mat. The concept is similar to that used in Victorian ferneries where porous tufa rock was kept moist for healthy fern growth. If a neighbor's wall is to be used, permission should be obtained first. Also, freestanding walls can be made using inexpensive cinder block.

A more traditional way of making a tapestry garden is to create tiers of planters attached by brackets to a wall, such as cradle planters and windowbox planters. At my own home, Cedaridge Farm, I still prefer the time-honored system

Ruined buildings were among Cézanne's favorite subjects, for they suggested mankind's vulnerability to nature. This ruined wall at Cedaridge Farm, Pennsylvania, is part of a barn that burned down in a thunderstorm, and then became a decorative garden accent. The idea of using the ruin as a decorative wall was inspired by Cézanne's painting of his own garden (see page 22).

of using tender plants (like Swedish ivy) at the top of a wall to drape down from windowboxes, elevated planters of ivy-leaf geraniums and Australian fan flowers to provide tiers of color midway up the wall, and tall plants like cannas to connect the bottom with the middle ground, so that the vertical curtain effect is achieved without the need for a felt liner, recirculating pump, and hydroponic nutrient solution.

The success of vertical walls depends to a large extent on foliage contrasts, for instance mixing straplike leaves with heart-shaped leaves, to create a tapestry of texture and form. The effect is especially attractive when color is subdued: use flowering plants sparsely. It's also important to realize that the top of a wall may have much brighter light than the bottom, and so the bottom may benefit from being planted with shade-loving plants, like maidenhair ferns and hostas. Although vertical gardens are ideal for introducing tropical plants, like spider plants and philodendron vines, one can reduce maintenance considerably by choosing hardy varieties. A surprising number of hardy plants can introduce a tropical flavor—feathery maidenhair ferns, Japanese painted ferns, and velvety piggyback plants (*Tolmeia menziesii*), for example.

Although the use of tropical plants does considerably expand one's creativity, wall gardens using hardy plants exclusively can remain in place for more than ten years without substantial renovation. Except for a spring cleanup and pruning to keep plants within bounds, an automatic watering and fertilizing system can ensure minimum maintenance, including little or no weeding.

Example of a "green wall" at Cedaridge Farm, Pennsylvania, a planting inspired by the luxuriant vibrancy of Cézanne's landscape paintings in which the sense of perspective is drastically reduced. Heart-shaped moonflower vine and parasol-shaped nasturtium leaves contrast with the arching leaves of spider plants and an avalanche of button-shaped leaves of bacopa, shimmering with tiny white flowers. Pink and red vining geraniums also add decorative touches.

TREE ACCENTS

Several of Cézanne's paintings focus on a particular tree in the landscape, such as the *Large Pine
Tree Near Aix* (1890–95), *The Large Pine* (1889),
and *Pistachio Tree in the Courtyard of the Château
Noir* (1900). The administration of Cézanne's
garden today makes a feature of several large
trees, in particular a chestnut, a redbud, and a
sycamore with marbled bark. In garden settings
tree accents are especially appealing when they
have richly colored bark that contrasts well with
green foliage. Two of the best include white
birch (*Betula papyrifera*) and paperbark maple
(*Acer griseum*).

Paul *Cézanne*, Large Pine and Red Earth; *Hermitage Museum, St. Petersburg. The radiating branches of this mature Aleppo pine, along the route du Tholonet, echo the lines of a similar pine at the bottom of Cézanne's garden.*

Mature ponderosa pine overlooking a New Zealand lake emulates the power and majesty of Cézanne's painting, showing how a single tree in the garden can create a dramatic, dominant focal point, as in the natural landscape.

Sycamore tree with mottled bronze-and-green bark lights up the tree canopy in Cézanne's garden today. Other fine landscape trees with decorative bark include the New England white birch, the copperbark cherry, and paperbark maple.

Paul Cézanne, Avenue at Chantilly; *Toledo Museum of Art, Ohio. This is one of Cézanne's best paintings of a "leaf tunnel," featuring the façade of a château framed by the tall trunks and arching branches of deciduous trees. The inclusion of the building gives the avenue of trees a true sense of scale.*

LEAF TUNNELS

Another foliage effect evident in Cézanne's paintings is the leaf tunnel. Rather than a flat curtain of color, it presents more depth and a focal point, which can be a building framed by the foliage or a path leading off into infinity.

Cézanne was drawn to woodland and especially woodland gravel roads or plain dirt paths patterned by shadows, though he also admired grand avenues of sycamores and chestnuts lining country roads and driveways leading to imposing châteaus. The Jas de Bouffan's wide, tree-lined avenue is a feature in several of Cézanne's paintings. The artist presented them with strongly erect flared trunks and branches that meet to create a vaulted canopy like the nave of a cathedral.

Today the predominant garden design feature at Les Lauves is a series of woodland paths that wind through groves of shrubs and trees to create leafy tunnels. In addition to pines, chestnuts, and sycamores, there are such smaller trees as redbuds, olives, mock oranges, and figs, the lower branches pruned away to show beautiful bark textures on the trees and a tracery of branches from the multiple trunks of shrubs.

Woodland scenes are Cézanne's most frequent subject, and two paintings that show the best leaf tunnel effects are *Road to Mas Jolie at the Château Noir* (1895—1900), showing a wide, straight path leading through the forest, and *Avenue at Chantilly* (1888), featuring a bridle path leading through chestnut trees and forming a window that frames the blue mansard roofs of the Chantilly château. The main difference between the two motifs is that one features a building as its focal point, while the other leads off into a mysterious unknown.

Nothing in a landscape provides a sense of place more definitely than trees. Majestic live oaks shrouded in Spanish moss immediately identify the American South; coconut palms a South Sea island; avenues of stout oak an English landscape. Streets lined with sycamores or chestnuts are synonymous with Provence, and olive trees identify a Mediterranean climate.

The effect of a tunnel of trees can be enhanced in many ways—by decorative bark (like the green-and-gray marbling of sycamores), by a distinctive leaf canopy (like the feathery leaflets of locust and silk trees), and by a profusion of flowers (as with chestnuts and redbuds) or a stunning autumn leaf coloration (as with poplars and sugar maples). Even the wandlike silhouettes of closely spaced bamboo and mock orange can make beautiful tunnels. Strategically placed along paths, they can become a visual adventure.

In creating a leafy tunnel or avenue, it's important to consider the mature height and width of the tree and its rate of growth. In England wealthy landowners often planted double rows of trees—a foreground row of a fast-growing, short-lived variety to give an early effect, and a rear row of slower-growing spreading oaks to take over. Some of the most impressive *grands allées* can be seen at Versailles Palace. Even though a recent storm felled ten thousand trees, the grandeur of those that remain is still awesome. Many of these are beech trees, which are too slow-growing and too big for most modern properties.

ABOVE

This château, along the route du Tholonet, close to Cézanne's garden, is framed by a wide avenue of sycamore trees and exquisite water reflections from a canal.

BELOW

Entrance to a vineyard near Cézanne's garden, showing beautiful shadow patterns slanting across the gravel drive, and parallel hedges of clipped boxwood creating a bold contrast to the burgeoning growth of chestnut trees.

GARDEN STRUCTURE

When Cézanne hired Mourgues to design his studio at Les Lauves, he wanted a structure that would blend unobtrusively with the pristine landscape beyond its boundary walls; he was unhappy with the ostentatious polished wood and fanciful mosaics the architect added. What he wanted was a studio like the Château Noir of his paintings—an architectonic structure that seemed to be an outgrowth of the mountain itself. He desired a fusion of man and nature, an integration of house and garden that would be soothing to his senses.

All too often it is the architect who has design control of both the house and garden. He or she may employ a landscape architect or a plantsperson to help with filling the garden space, but the architect often designs a garden loaded with hardscape elements such as rills and arbors, retaining walls and showy fountains, bridges and gazebos. Consequently, the garden ends up being an extension of the house, and the two sometimes assert themselves harshly over the natural terrain. Cézanne wanted his house to fuse with the landscape, as does Frank Lloyd Wright's Fallingwater in Bear Run, Pennsylvania—the house cantilevered over a waterfall like shelves of rock.

In France today a garden that blends architectural integrity with sensitive garden design reminiscent of the paintings of Cézanne is Kerdalo, the Brittany home of the late Prince Wolkonsky and now maintained by his daughter, Isabelle Vaughan. Her father discovered the sheltered coastal valley, with acid-rich soil, near the port town of Tregeure and set out to establish a beautiful garden that would also complement the stonemason's art. Though the buildings seem to be fifteenth-century, they date to only 1962, when the prince, in his sixties, concentrated his creative skills as a painter, architect, stonemason, and gardener to produce a unique marriage of house and landscape in the Cézanne tradition. A large garden facing the English Channel, Kerdalo seamlessly combines woodland and water, boggy land and dry slopes, trees,

LEFT

In Cézanne's landscape paintings the contrast between robust old buildings and luxurious foliage is a favorite theme. This beautiful partnership of plants and stone at Kerdalo, in Brittany, was begun in 1962 when the late owner, Prince Wolkowsky, combined his talents as a painter, architect, stonemason, and gardener to create a château that seems to belong to the fifteenth century.

ABOVE

House of the Hanged Man, *as it exists today, showing a slight lean to one of the gables, which Cézanne emphasized in his painting.*

LEFT

Paul Cézanne, The House of the Hanged Man; *Musée d'Orsay, Paris. This landscape painting of a house on a hillside overlooking Auvers, near Paris, was sold at an early Impressionist Exhibition, where work by Monet and Renoir failed to sell.*

shrubs, and perennials with exquisite stonework, including a tower that resembles Cézanne's structure in *The House of the Hanged Man* and was constructed largely from old stone and old woodwork cannibalized from ruined buildings.

Trees were planted not only to shelter the property from gales but also to create a tapestry effect and cathedrals of greenery. For skyline effect there is even a grove of mature Chilean monkey puzzle trees; while other grand gardens may have one or two, at Kerdalo more than a dozen lend a prehistoric aura to the crest of a hill.

The house sits not on the highest point but snugly nestled midway down the valley, between a sunny slope and a sweeping lawn vista coursed by a meandering stream. The sunny slope is terraced and the drought-tolerant plantings present a verdant backdrop of mostly subtropical species, such as elegant spires of giant lobelia (*Echium pininana*), spiky purple spires of New Zealand flax (*Phormium tenax*), and billowing bushes of blue California lilac (*Ceanothus impressus*).

A *bridle path at Kerdalo, Brittany, leading through woodland, with shade-loving hydrangeas and yellow hypericum adding subdued splashes of color to a leafy tunnel. Cézanne painted hydrangeas underneath an archway of trees at the Jas de Bouffan.*

Detail of a tapestry garden at Kerdalo, Brittany, showing how the foliage of trees and shrubs can mingle to paint a landscape in myriad leaf tones. What looks like a white-flowering tree is actually a variegated pagoda dogwood, producing a shimmering-white contrast to trees with mostly green, blue, yellow, and bronze foliage.

Millstone used as a garden ornament at Deerfield Garden, Pennsylvania, with English ivy decorating the surrounding wall and ground. Cézanne wrote that when choosing a composition he looked for certain geometric shapes in nature as a guide, especially the sphere (represented here by the millstone), as well as the cylinder and the cone.

Level with the house is an extraordinary tapestry garden using trees and shrubs with gold, silver, and all shades of green foliage to create a Cézanne landscape. Below the house the stream ensures a moist environment for a rich collection of Himalayan rhododendrons, New Zealand tree ferns, feathery astilbes, and Chilean rhubarb with gigantic velvetlike leaves. But almost always—as in Cézanne's images of Mont Sainte-Victoire landscapes—the plants veil beautiful stone structures, such as a pair of belvederes marking the limits of a sunken garden, a grotto with pebble mosaics and a cascade, and a faux moat with towering stone walls garlanded with vines.

Cézanne knew better than anyone that the design and placement of buildings in a pristine landscape need not be visually destructive. He deplored the desecration of one of his favorite motifs—the beautiful coastal town of L'Estaque—through the erection of ugly factories, sprawling quays, high-rise buildings, and gasworks; at the other extreme he marveled at the way the Château Noir beside the route du Tholonet embellished nature, with a façade and roofline that matched the red-ochre clay of the mountain it faced, and a secret courtyard with an ancient pistachio tree at its center. He doted on the château's wide, gravelly garden terraces decorated with quarry stones, millstones, circular stone cisterns, and nature paths leading off into cathedrals of indigenous greenery.

A *garden combining natural rocky outcrops with plants noted for strong foliage contrasts, including English ivy, hostas, and ostrich ferns, reminiscent of Cézanne's landscape paintings.*

M *oss-covered rocks and an ivy-girdled tree display the kind of wild natural beauty Cézanne admired and wanted for his garden.*

SEE-THROUGH PLANTS

A curious aspect of Cézanne's landscape paintings is the lack of flowers, especially when one considers the number of wildflower meadows painted by other Impressionists and post-Impressionists—lavender fields by van Gogh and poppy fields by Monet, for example. Vast fields of wildflowers cover the slopes of Mont Sainte-Victoire in spring and summer, yet Cézanne never chose them as a motif. Flowers are not completely absent from his landscapes, but generally they are used as incidental foreground elements, for veiling the main subject of his composition. Another term for a plant used for veiling is *see-through plant*.

Cézanne uses plants as a veil in many of his paintings, notably *The Pool at Jas de Bouffan* (1878–79) and *Woods* (1894), but the most striking example of Cézanne's rendering of see-through

plants is an early Impressionistic work showing a waterside garden near Paris entitled *House of Père Lacroix at Auvers* (1873), in which the house is seen through a veil of what appears to be yellow broom and airy panicles of blue lilac blossoms.

The concept of using see-through plants to embellish gardens has only recently caught on in Europe and the United States, thanks to their use by several Dutch garden designers, including artist Ton ter Linden and nurseryman Piet Oudolf, both of whom use them in exquisite perennial gardens.

A see-through flowering plant can be annual, biennial, or perennial. It must offer an arrangement of flower stems or decorative leaves that are airy, slender, or glittery, enabling viewers to see through them in border plantings, producing the sensation of vibration. See-through plants include easy-to-grow annuals such as annual fleabane (*Erigeron annuus*), white baby's breath (*Gypsophila elegans*), and vervain (*Verbena bonariensis*). Also good choices are some easy-to-grow perennials such as feathery silver spires of wormwood (*Artemisia ludoviciana*), wands of bronze fennel, and loose spikes of jupiter's beard (*Centranthus ruber*) with mostly pink flowers that can look like clouds of pink smoke wafting into the stratosphere. Biennials are rich in see-through plants, notably *Verbascum olympicum*, with tall candelabra-like wands studded with yellow flowers, and *Salvia sclarea*, with sprays of pink, papery flowers. Both grow wild on the slopes of Mont Sainte-Victoire.

See-through plants are best used in front of richly textured surfaces, such as weathered barn siding or a wall of rough fieldstone. How appealing it is to have steeples of pink foxgloves, wands of white snakeroot, powder-blue veronica stabbing the sky, and poppies waving their delicate petals in the breeze, the contrasting textured background surface clearly visible through the veil of petals. But unlike Monet, who used see-through plants lavishly throughout his Giverny garden, Cézanne used them sparingly, for his main objective was a garden of more durable design elements—stonework, foliage effects, and woody plant forms.

Beautiful example of a French tapestry garden, seen at the Parc Floral de Moutiers, near Varengeville, Normandy. The garden's founder was a collector of Impressionist art and used swatches of fabric to "paint" the landscape with foliage colors akin to the landscapes of Cézanne's paintings. Here, an old oak tree is used as a strong focal point, its stout trunk and radiating branches similar to Cézanne's Large Pine and Red Earth (*see page 76*).

GARDENS OF THE MACABRE

Cézanne was a devout Roman Catholic who attended mass every Sunday and believed that a religious upbringing helped develop a good moral character. Though he considered himself a prude, paradoxically much of Cézanne's work is devoted to violence, death, and sexuality. He painted still lifes incorporating human skulls, and his renderings of the Jas de Bouffan have a sinister appearance, some of his paintings, such as *Pool and Fountain at the Jas de Bouffan* (1888–90), presenting the garden as though it were a graveyard.

The Les Lauves studio even today features Christ on a crucifix above a pyramid of human skulls, and it is not much of a stretch to see how Cézanne would have delighted in seeing a garden combining religious elements and symbols of death in a similar morbid design. Indeed, there are gardens today that deliberately present a sinister, almost supernatural appearance by combining religious and macabre artifacts. Many are cemetery gardens, where trees are allowed to grow into ghoulish shapes, and gravestones featuring skulls and crossbones enhance the feeling of a grim and gruesome place. Completely at home in a cemetery garden would be Cézanne's *Pistachio Tree in the Courtyard of the Château Noir* (1900), showing the ancient, weathered tree growing through limestone blocks resembling tombstones, one of which appears to be a discarded carved wellhead.

A provocative ornament sometimes seen in secret gardens and intended to shock visitors represents Leda and the Swan, of Greek mythology. Displayed as a sculpture or as a wall frieze along garden walks, the sight of a naked Leda being ravished by Zeus in the form of a swan is bound to raise eyebrows. At England's Hever Castle, Edenbridge, for example, a small Leda sculpture occupying a wall niche in the Italian garden, near the swan lake, closely

matches Cézanne's portrayal of the story in his painting entitled *Leda with the Swan* (1886–90). It is typical of a whole series of erotic or titillating subjects that he stopped painting after he married Hortense Fiquet.

At Eleutherian Mills, the historic home of the founder of the DuPont chemical dynasty, there is a spectacular folly garden—known as the Crowninshield Garden—designed to evoke a Roman ruin, the ruined walls and columns erected on wooded terraces descending a slope. There are secret passages with cobblestone floors, a boxwood garden featuring a wall frieze with the head of Medusa, and a statue of David holding the severed head of Goliath. These features, along with artifacts from the old mills, including rusting cogwheels and massive metal cauldrons once used to mix gunpowder, create motifs similar to those Cézanne painted at the Château Noir.

Cézanne liked to encounter ruins in the landscape, for it showed nature's ability to reclaim mankind's intrusion. This explains his obsession with the grounds of the Château Noir, a property featuring an overgrown, neglected garden. Though this ruin seems authentic, it is in fact a clever garden folly designed to resemble a historic Roman ruin, created by the late Frank Crowninshield when he lived at Eleutherian Mills, the family seat of the DuPont chemical dynasty, near Wilmington, Delaware.

A CÉZANNE-STYLE GARDEN

This small-space planting plan—intended to evoke an eerie, supernatural aura—shows garden design elements that Cézanne most admired. To create a Cézanne-inspired garden, begin with a wall, preferably ruined and covered with English ivy. To create a sense of the macabre, decorate a window space or other niche with skulls, and add a nude figure (such as this one, of Leda and the Swan) along the back for shock value. Echo the geometric shapes Cézanne admired in nature (the sphere, the cylinder, and the cone) by creating a tableau of spherical river stones on a slab table, or adding a small, spherical water lily pool, a cone-shaped arch of Oriental bamboo, or even cylindrical fallen columns. Contrast the

geometric shapes with the sinuous lines of a Japanese cut-leaf maple, pruned to emphasize its dark, branch silhouettes. To suggest that nature is reclaiming man's orderly dominion, you might have an ivy-girdled tree; a blazing red hydrangea that offers a discordant floral accent; a path of broken flagstones leading to a substantial stone bench; and an olive jar planter, deliberately cracked to reinforce a sense of man's vulnerability to nature. In a clearing before the ruin add fragrant low-growing herbs—cushions of thyme, lavender, and rosemary that release spicy aromas—that Cézanne admired on his walks in the surrounding countryside.

Though this garden will fit into a space 25 ft. by 25 ft., it can be adapted to fill a larger space.

CHAPTER SIX

STILL-LIFE ARRANGEMENT AND FAVORITE PLANTS

Give me an apple and I will conquer Paris.

—CÉZANNE, EXPLAINING THE ABILITY OF
AN APPLE TO REVEAL ARTISTIC SKILL

OPPOSITE

Cluster of geraniums in pots at
Les Lauves, a favorite Cézanne
motif. He particularly liked their
bold, ruffled leaves, and sometimes
painted the plants without
flowers.

WHEN CÉZANNE was asked to name his favorite flower, he surprised everyone by naming scabiosa, for his paintings of potted and vining ivy-leaf geraniums were greatly admired. All of the Impressionist painters had favorite flowers that they painted as garden subjects or still-life arrangements. Henri Fantin-Latour and Renoir cherished roses, and both had rose varieties named in their honor while they were living. Monet created one of the most extensive private collections of water lilies in order to paint them; van Gogh declared the sunflower his own. Manet used a vase of pink and red peonies to show how effectively a heavy impasto application of paint could capture the sensation of luscious petals when the colors were applied with a palette knife. Though the critics hated Manet's peonies, both Cézanne and van Gogh were inspired to use the same technique—van Gogh in his rendition of sunflower still lifes and Cézanne in some of his family portraits and still lifes of fruit.

Flower subjects were popular with the public and often were the first canvases to sell at exhibition. The painting of flowers also helped the Impressionists in their exploration of technique. Cut flowers were good subjects to paint on rainy days in the comfort of a studio when it was difficult to paint outdoors.

Boston ivy used to soften a monotonous expanse of wall facing a courtyard in Eguisheim, Alsace. The cascading vines of ivy-leaf geraniums spill from a window box, creating the type of informal, understated beauty Cézanne greatly admired.

PAGES 98–99

The hardy perennial scabiosa 'Pink Mist' massed with blue salvia and blue perennial geranium. 'Pink Mist' also blooms nonstop from spring to autumn frost.

RIGHT

The hardy perennial scabiosa 'Butterfly Blue' flowers nonstop from spring until autumn frost.

Scabiosa is a popular hardy perennial in French gardens, especially *Scabiosa caucasica*, which is noted for mostly flat, blue ruffled flower heads. It not only produces a good floral display in the garden but has long wiry stems suitable for cutting. Commonly called pincushion flower for a raised cushion of white calyces at the center, the variety 'Clive Grieve' is a popular large-flowered light blue, with individual flowers up to three inches across. 'Fama' is a deep blue, while 'Alba' is a beautiful white. These varieties, growing three feet tall, mostly bloom in midsummer.

Another perennial scabiosa, *S. columbaria*, only slightly smaller-flowered than *S. caucasica*, blooms nonstop from spring until heavy autumn frosts. 'Butterfly Blue' and 'Pink Mist' are extremely popular varieties because they are low-growing and can be used for bedding.

Annual scabiosa are easily grown from seed sown directly into the garden. They are fast-growing in full sun and have the largest color range, not only blue and white but also pink, red, purple, and black. The flowers are generally more rounded than the perennial types and also popular for both mass bedding and cutting.

CÉZANNE'S STILL LIFES

Ernest Quost was a reputable Parisian painter of flowers. His particular favorite was the hollyhock, and he beautifully portrayed the iridescent sheen of its silklike petals. After viewing Cézanne's first one-man exhibition, he sought out Cézanne's dealer, Ambroise Vollard, and complained bitterly: "Flowers! Flowers! Has your painter ever even looked at a flower? How many years, monsieur, have I, who stand before you now, spent in intimate communion with the flower? You know what my friends call me, monsieur? The Corot of the Flower."

What Quost failed to realize is that many of Cézanne's still-life arrangements were metaphorical landscapes. A spill of fruit represents a rock fall, the folds of fabric the contours of a mountain, crockery and other props architecture. Even black clocks, conch shells, and skulls introduce the favorite geometric forms of his landscapes. Similarly, his choice of flower was intended not so much to show a recognizable variety but to provide desirable color, balance, and form.

Quost was a celebrated painter. Even van Gogh declared that nobody could paint a hollyhock as well as Quost, but Quost's realistic flower paintings did not sell as well as Cézanne's, and he felt frustrated over Cézanne's highly stylized, elemental approach to flower paintings in which the observer often had difficulty telling what type of flower was depicted. "Oh! Corollas, stamens, calyces, stems, pistils, stigmas, pollen, how many times have I drawn them and painted them," Quost said. "More than three thousand studies of detail, monsieur, before even daring to attack the humblest flower of the field! And I can't sell them. But your Cézanne painted that from paper flowers, didn't he?" Vollard had to admit it.

Cézanne used flowers to explore form and color sensations in ways that too much detail would destroy. Joris-Karl Huysmans, the art critic, analyzing one of Cézanne's apple arrangements, declared that "all his life, he sought a personal style capable of imbuing the most humble subjects with nobility . . . these paintings [are] pioneers if we compare them to elegantly traditional still lifes."

One of Cézanne's most important small-scale arrangements is entitled *The Blue Vase* (1883–87). In this case the focus is an upright deep blue vase with a narrow neck and fluted rim. The flowers, which include sky-blue Dutch irises, are incidental and serve to heighten the extraordinary blue of the vase, while a pale blue background helps to intensify the blueness of the vase even more strongly. Also significant is a mass of gold coloring representing the tabletop, creating a distinctive blue-and-gold color harmony.

A floral arrangement inspired by Cézanne's still-life painting The Blue Vase *(displayed today at the Musée d'Orsay, Paris), showing Dutch irises and peonies grouped in a vase with a cluster of fruit on a table.*

CÉZANNE'S FAVORITE PLANTS

Flowers are notably absent from Cézanne's landscape and garden scenes, where trees and shrubs always take precedence, and the more animated the tree, the better he liked it. When he considered purchasing the property of Les Lauves for his studio, it was the gnarled old olive trees and contorted fig trees that aided his decision. Glittering apple blossoms, pencil-straight poplars, pines with strong radiating branches, spirelike junipers, billowing chestnuts and lilacs, sometimes the focus and sometimes the accompaniment—these are painted more than any other objects.

Flowers are presented mostly in arrangements. When he visited the art critic Gustave Geffroy to paint his portrait in his library, Cézanne took with him a pink rose to place in a bud vase for the sitter to contemplate. He painted geraniums with vigorous vining stems and leaves, even without flowers, as in *Potted Plants (Geraniums)* (1888–90). When he painted flowers themselves, they tended to be blowsy—large peonies, luscious roses, bold hydrangeas, and dinner-plate dahlias—or to possess an interesting petal structure, like the blue Dutch irises in *The Blue Vase*. A still life of Dutch bulbs, entitled *Tulips and Apples* (1890–94), shows red lily-flowered tulips, with pointed, reflexed petals, and daffodils recognizable as an old-fashioned variety called 'Pheasant's Eye.' Though the tulips and daffodils are garden flowers, Cézanne has tempered their cultivated look with sprigs of wild buttercups. In another powerful still life, *Bouquet of Yellow Dahlias* (1873), a group of garden-variety annual dahlias is the main focus of the arrangement, but Cézanne includes a spray of wayside grasses and wildflowers in the background to soften the highly bred appearance of the dahlias.

Cézanne's need to soften the effect of cultivated flowers was shared by Monet, who encouraged wild oxeye daisies and poppies to grow liberally among plantings of hybrid irises, dahlias, and peonies, and who referred to his wildflowers as "the soul of the garden."

A *still-life arrangement featuring lily-flowered tulips and 'Pheasant's Eye' daffodils, inspired by Cézanne's painting* Tulips and Apples, *owned by the Art Institute of Chicago.*

OPPOSITE

'P*heasant's Eye' daffodils blooming today in a French garden, the Clos Coudray, near Rouen. An heirloom variety still offered by bulb merchants, the small rimmed center cup is pleasantly fragrant. Cézanne's painting style captured in oils the way the flared petals are swept back as though the flowers are in flight.*

CHAPTER SEVEN

MONT SAINTE-VICTOIRE AND LA ROCHE-GUYON

In the mythology of modernism, Cézanne is a kind of Moses figure who wandered for years in a wilderness (the sunstruck landscape of Provence), went to the mountain (his beloved Mont Sainte-Victoire), and then glimpsed the promised land of abstract painting.

—JOSEPH SKRAPITS, DIVERSIONS MAGAZINE

OPPOSITE
Mont Sainte-Victoire
in early-morning mist.

OST VISITORS TO Cézanne's garden congregate on his patio and join a slow-moving line to enter the house, and afterward they wander the paths beyond the terrace, but relatively few ever take the two roads that skirt the majestic heights of Mont Sainte-Victoire, which is a pity. If you do not take the time to follow in Cézanne's footsteps in the shadow of the mountain, it's difficult to appreciate the magic of his garden. Metaphorically speaking, the mountain *is* his garden, while Les Lauves is the accompaniment, for even when he painted the cultivated space within the walls of his garden, he invariably included a view of the mountain—a view that today is unfortunately obscured by high-rise buildings and screens of trees.

In Cézanne's day, whether he was living at the Jas de Bouffan, on the western edge of Aix, or at Les Lauves, on its northern edge, he would either walk to view the mountain or take a ride by cart or rental car. Even today the edge of town quickly gives way to bucolic countryside, and the roads that encircle the mountain are little changed from the time Cézanne traveled them. Circling the mountain by car in an hour or two, the visitor can easily understand why Sainte-Victoire was such a magical place for Cézanne. After two days of leisurely exploring I had still hardly scratched its surface, and I felt its pull as Cézanne must have felt it, wishing to explore every ravine, sketch every rock formation, and hike every dirt track leading to its summit. Its pervasive beauty fully justifies a description by the Parisian art collector Victor

Paul Cézanne, Montagne Sainte-Victoire; *Courtauld Institute Gallery, London. This view of the mountain from the route du Tholonet shows the Château Noir barely visible in the forested middle ground.*

View looking down from the heights of Mont Sainte-Victoire, old weathered pines silhouetted against morning mist like the pine-clad cliffs of Japan's Inland Sea.

Choquet when he visited Cézanne in 1886 and declared, "This region is full of undiscovered treasures." He felt that nobody before Cézanne had proved worthy of the "riches that lie slumbered here."

A good way to explore the mountain today is to take Cézanne's favorite route, known as route du Tholonet (route Cézanne), which winds through foothills toward the picturesque town of Gardanne, where Cézanne lived for a year after his son was born. Because he and the boy's mother were not married, he kept his domestic relationship a secret. He would come from the Jas de Bouffan to visit Hortense and his son every day at Gardanne when they were not ensconced in Paris.

Along the route are large umbrella pines of the kind Cézanne painted, their branches framing or veiling a distant panorama of fields and mountain. High on a hill, above the pines, are still visible the beige walls and red roofs of buildings he painted, including those of the Château Noir.

After the château the road descends to the small community of Le Tholonet, where Cézanne liked to eat at the Restaurant Berne. A magnificent avenue of sycamore trees leads to the Château Tholonet, now used as government offices, and just a mile beyond, on a rise beyond the road, is the tower of a stone windmill from where Cézanne painted the mountain. Picnic tables provide a good place to rest and admire the view, for through the trees the countryside is a patchwork of orchards and agricultural fields bounded by fieldstone walls, the plowed earth matching the color of the orange-red rooftops. A side road by the mill leads to a small park beside a cemetery. From the parking area a lumber trail leads to a rocky ridge reminiscent of Cézanne's numerous motifs combining rock formations and pines.

Back on the main road a sunny landscape opens out, with cart tracks leading off on both sides to small farmsteads, their verges often decorated with sweeps of wildflowers. Prominent in spring are deep blue bearded irises with blue-green sword-shaped leaves, colonies of pink vervain growing in gravel, and spires of yellow verbascum and pink salvia jutting skyward.

Streams cascading from the mountain create a series of waterfalls beside the road. To the left the land is often scrubby, rocky, and eroded, run-off from the mountain carving deep ravines in the red clay. To the right the land is more heavily forested, and as the road begins an uphill climb through trees, there is a park sign announcing the start of a trail leading to Cézanne's Cabin, a stone structure providing shelter at a spot where Cézanne liked to paint boulders and trees. The rough, stony trail leads up the slopes of Mont Sainte-Victoire, rocky ridges topped by lines of umbrella pines. In places the scene is reminiscent of a Japanese landscape, with pines twisted into bonsai shapes by the wind and harsh terrain. A potpourri of herbal scents pervades the atmosphere from wild bush rosemary, Spanish broom, clumps of lavender, and cushions of thyme. The landscape is like an enormous rock garden, buzzing with bees, its powerful rock formations harboring an array of plants inured to lashings of rain, constant winds, and long periods of summer drought.

BELOW

Dirt road leading to a small farmhouse along the route du Tholonet. Cézanne painted many of the ochre-colored châteaus and farmhouses on the slopes of Mont Sainte-Victoire.

PAGES 112–113

Avenue of sycamore trees along the route du Tholonet, featured in Cézanne's paintings.

One afternoon while exploring the ravines near Cézanne's Cabin, I failed to see dark thunderheads envelop the mountain, and soon I was drenched in sheets of cold rain that caused a dense mist to swirl up from the hot stones, hiding the trail. It was hard to keep my bearings; all I could do was to scramble blindly downhill, barely able to see my feet, stumbling over loose stones and stunted bushes, knowing that at some point I would come to the road. It was easy to visualize Cézanne, at age sixty-seven, being caught in a similar storm, becoming disoriented from the lack of visibility, and eventually falling victim to the pneumonia that would cause his death. Fortunately for me, the deluge lifted soon enough for me to reach my car without mishap.

The sun broke through and I continued along the main road, which zigzags uphill steeply, then levels out and again parallels the eastern flank of the mountain, past the Château Mont Sainte-Victoire to a progressively less populated landscape of valleys with views clear to the Mediterranean coast. Miles upon miles of desolate country roads lead off in all directions—to Gardanne, where Cézanne painted nine oils and two watercolors of the town, and beyond to L'Estaque, a coastal community that yielded thirty-three oils and five watercolors. Cézanne had a special fondness for L'Estaque, admiring the way its red roofs contrasted with the blue of the Mediterranean, backed by high, hazy mountains on a distant promontory. He lived there at various times between 1864 and 1887. Eventually, however, as L'Estaque grew from a quiet fishing village into a bustling industrial suburb of Marseilles, Cézanne could not bear to see it marred by industrial blight.

Though the route du Tholonet provides the best views of Cézanne's mountain, an alternative route is the Cours des Arts et Métiers, the road to Vauvenargues. It has the advantage of being the only road that provides access to a favorite Cézanne subject, the Carrière de Bibemus or Bibemus Quarry. The Vauvenargues road twists and winds along a beautiful valley, threading its way between darkly wooded slopes above, on the mountain side, and sunny meadows below, following the mountain's western flanks. Several miles out of Aix there is a turning to the right leading to the quarry, where Cézanne completed eleven oils and sixteen watercolors and rented a cabin to store his paintings. The parking lot for the quarry is next to the parking lot for the nearby François Zola Dam, built by Emile Zola's father.

Access to the quarry itself is along a dirt road at the far end of the parking lot, and though the quarry is abandoned, the ochre-colored stone and the stonecutter's marks on the cliffs are still recognizable as the motif for Cézanne's most famous quarry painting, *The Bibemus Quarry* (1895). Complex shadows play across the cliffs of the quarry; it was these shadow patterns on the large natural and man-made blocks of stone that appealed to him as a mostly orange and blue color harmony. At the crest of the quarry are mature pines sculptured by the wind and nature trails that rim a deep ravine formed by the river Arc. It's also possible to walk across the top of the dam and view its scenic reservoir.

Vauvanargues village provides scenic views

of the Château Vauvanargues, where Picasso is buried beneath a tall cedar that towers above the main courtyard. Beyond the village, the road arrives at a parking area with a trail that provides access to the peaks of Mont Sainte-Victoire and a cross marking its summit. The road then joins the route du Tholonet, completing a circuit through what is still one of the most picturesque and unspoiled parts of France.

Another interesting side trip that provides recognizable Cézanne motifs is the Maison Bellevue, west of Aix. From 1886 Cézanne's sister Rose and her husband owned this property, which provided Cézanne with a vast panoramic view of the mountain across the Vallée de l'Arc.

An example of the red clay found on the slopes of Mont Sainte-Victoire, which featured prominently in Cézanne's landscape paintings.

Spanning the river Arc is a viaduct that became the subject of Cézanne's most glorious landscape painting, *Mont Sainte-Victoire Seen from Bellevue* (1885). A total of eleven oils and sixteen watercolors were painted from this vantage point. (Bellevue is the house that Renoir rented at the end of 1889 when he visited Cézanne in Aix and found the Jas de Bouffan too dismal to stay in.)

CÉZANNE AT LA ROCHE-GUYON

The quaint Normandy village of La Roche-Guyon is situated beside the river Seine northwest of Paris. There used to be a bridge there, but during the Nazi occupation of France in World War II it was destroyed and never replaced. During his visits to Paris, Cézanne liked to visit the village to paint, and some summers he rented a house close to the river. Renoir also liked the village and rented a summer house on the rue des Jardins. Monet rented a riverside property four miles upstream at Vétheuil; he eventually settled just three miles downstream at Giverny, where his restored garden is located.

The village of La Roche-Guyon is little changed since the days Cézanne explored its streets and beautiful countryside. The ruins of an ancient castle that repelled invasions by Romans and Vikings dominate the landscape, crowning a high hill overlooking the village. Cézanne painted the castle and below it an imposing château, which the German army commander General Field Marshal Rommel commandeered for his headquarters during the Nazi occupation. Driving back to the château from a troop inspection following the Normandy invasion, his car was strafed by an Allied

Ruined fortress over-looking the community of La Roche-Guyon. Cézanne painted the ruin and during summer often rented a house in the village as a base for painting excursions.

fighter plane. His driver was killed and Rommel suffered severe injuries to his head, with fractures to his skull, temple, and jaw and shrapnel in his left eye.

Rommel, who admired Impressionist art, had previously visited Monet's house and garden, which was under the care of Monet's stepdaughter, Blanche, following her stepfather's death in 1926. During the occupation, Rommel inspected the household's cache of original Monet paintings, and though the house could have been requisitioned to billet soldiers, and the paintings stolen, he placed the property off-limits to assure the safety of Monet's work.

Cobbled street at the
center of La Roche-Guyon;
many of its houses cloaked
in English ivy and Virginia
creeper, which turns red in
autumn. Cézanne, Monet,
and Renoir all explored
its streets and surrounding
countryside in search of
landscapes to paint.

118

One of Cézanne's most important canvases of the village is *A Turn in the Road at La Roche-Guyon* (1885), showing the main road as it runs from Giverny, descending a steep hill toward the village. The castle can be seen in the background, the château below it facing the Seine, and in the foreground is a sheer cliff face with entrances to man-made limestone caves. During the Nazi occupation, many local inhabitants fled to these caves; they emerged after liberation "white as chicory," according to one observer.

This house beside the main road leading into La Roche-Guyon is covered in Virginia creeper and autumn colors, while evergreen English ivy cloaks the balustrade. This is the same building featured on the far right of Cézanne's A Turn in the Road at La Roche-Guyon (*Smith College Museum of Art, Northampton, Mass.*), *opposite. The ruined fortress shown on page 117 can be seen on the upper left.*

The village of Auvers is about thirty minutes southeast by car, near the Paris suburb of Pontoise. In appearance it is very similar to La Roche-Guyon, both villages backed by steep hills and cliffs. Auvers attracted artists for the beauty of its village and surrounding countryside. Landscape artist Charles Daubigny had a house in the village, and Vincent van Gogh lived three months there, under the care of Dr. Paul Gachet, an avid collector of Impressionist art.

Cézanne received treatment from the doctor for bouts of depression, and from the garden terraces of his home painted a high-elevation view of the countryside and rooftops of Auvers. He rented rooms directly across the street from the doctor. Of the two important paintings from Cézanne's explorations of Auvers, *The House of the Hanged Man* (1873) shows a view along a steep dirt lane toward an imposing stone house set among trees (see p. 82). The painting, shown at the first Impressionist Exhibition, was purchased by a discriminating collector and wealthy landowner, Compte Doria. Since few other painters enjoyed sales from this exhibition, its purchase was significant for Cézanne, not only for the satisfaction of making a worthwhile sale but as a mark of esteem among his compatriots whose work failed to sell.

The other significant painting from Cézanne's Auvers visits shows a house and garden. Entitled *House of Père Lacroix at Auvers* (1873), it features a snug red-roofed house veiled by blue lilacs and what appears to be a golden chain tree, the flowering trees reflected in a pond, and a steep wooded hillside in the background.

The streets of both La Roche-Guyon and Auvers feature beautiful terraced cottage gardens that present curtains of foliage contrasts. The hillsides abound with spring wildflowers, and even the golden chain tree (*Laburnum alpinum*) and pink butterfly bush (*Buddleia davidii*) grow wild in abundance on the rocky slopes.

OPPOSITE

View from the ruined fortress at La Roche-Guyon, showing a bend of the river Seine on the left, and the main road leading out of the village toward Giverny, in the next valley, where painter Claude Monet established his home and garden.

chronology

The name Cézanne is of Italian derivation. His art dealer, Ambroise Vollard, tells us that Cézanne's ancestors were peasants of Cesena, deeply religious and respectful of ancient tradition. When they left Italy to settle in France, they were known as the Cézannes, for their native town, and the name stuck. The following summary features the highlights of Paul Cézanne's career.

1839 Born January 19 at the rue de l'Opéra in Aix-en-Provence. His father, Louis-Auguste Cézanne, a hatter, and his mother, Anne-Elizabeth Aubert, were not married.

1841 Birth of his sister Marie.

1844 Marriage of his mother and father.

1844–50 Attends primary school in rue des Epineaux.

1848 Establishment of the Cézanne and Cabassol Bank.

1850–52 Pupil at the Saint Joseph Boarding School.

1852–58 Enters the Collège Bourbon. Establishes a friendship with Emile Zola.

1854 Birth of his second sister, Rose.

1857 Enrollment in the local art school in Aix, now the Granet Museum.

1858 Leaves for Paris but returns for summer holidays.

1859 Enrolls at the local law school at prompting of his father, who purchases the Jas de Bouffan (House of the Winds). Continues studies at local art school.

1861 Gives up his law studies. Leaves again for Paris and meets Pissarro at the Atelier Suisse art school. Discouraged, he returns to his father's bank but continues art classes locally.

1862 Leaves father's bank for good and returns to Paris. Joins Pissarro as an apprentice. Visits Pontoise, Auvers, La Roche-Guyon. Frequently visits the Louvre to copy masterpieces by Ingres, Courbet, Delacroix, and other leading French artists.

1863 Exhibits at the Salon des Refusés, in company with Pissarro, Monet, Renoir, and other Impressionist artists.

1864 After being rejected by the Paris Salon, returns to Aix.

1869 Meets his future wife, Hortense Fiquet, an artist's model at the Atelier Suisse, Paris.

1870 At the outbreak of the Franco-Prussian War takes refuge in L'Estaque, with Hortense.

1872 Birth of his son, Paul, with Hortense.

1874–76–77 Participates in the first, second, and third Impressionist Exhibitions, in Paris.

1882 Admitted to the Paris Salon for the only time in his career.

1883 Visited by Monet and Renoir in Aix-en-Provence.

1886 Following the publication of Zola's popular novel *L'Oeuvre* (in which the main character, modeled on Cézanne, is a disillusioned artist who commits suicide), Cézanne splits with his former close friend. Marries Hortense a month before his father's death.

1887 Rents a room at the Château Noir to store paintings while he paints its garden and the surrounding countryside.

1889 *The House of the Hanged Man* (1873) displayed at the Paris World's Fair in an exhibit of French art.

1895 Rents a cabin in the Bibemus Quarry, on Mont Sainte-Victoire, to store paintings. Art dealer Ambroise Vollard organizes the first one-man exhibit of Cézanne's work.

1897 Death of his mother.

1899 The Jas de Bouffan sold in order to settle his parents' estate with his two younger sisters. Fails to acquire Château Noir as a residence. Acquires an apartment in town at 23, rue Boulegon. Exhibits at the Salon des Indépendants, in Paris.

1901 Buys a plot of land on the chemin des Lauves and makes plans to build a studio, Les Lauves. Hires a gardener to tend its orchard of olive and fig trees and to make gardens around its perimeter.

1902 Death of Zola.

1906 Death of Cézanne, following his collapse on Mont Sainte-Victoire during a severe thunderstorm.

places to visit

HOW TO GET TO CÉZANNE'S GARDEN

Take one-way ring road around Aix Centre. At junction of boulevard Aristide Briand and avenue Pasteur, turn right up avenue Pasteur. Follow road to the right around hospital complex and turn right onto avenue Paul Cézanne. Cézanne's Garden and Studio is at 9, avenue Paul Cézanne on left, midway up the hill. For parking, continue past garden and take first right and first right again for entrance to parking lot. Also access by bus No. 1 from the Rotonde, Aix Centre.

Hours for Cézanne's Garden and Studio

October 1 to March 31: Open every day except December 25, January 1, and January 5, from 10 A.M. to 12 noon, then from 2 P.M. to 5 P.M.

April 1 to September 30: Open every day from 10 A.M. to 12 noon, then from 2:30 P.M. to 6 P.M.

OTHER PLACES OF INTEREST

France

MUSÉE GRANET

13100, place Saint-Jean de Malte, Aix-en-Provence.
Contains eight original Cézanne paintings, plus engravings, drawings, and a lithograph. Tel. 33 (0) 42 38 14 70.

MUSÉE D'ORSAY

62, rue de Lille, 75007 Paris.
Major collection of Cézanne's art, and other Impressionist painters. Tel. 33 (0) 1 40 49 48 14.

FOLLOWING IN CÉZANNE'S FOOTSTEPS

At 9 A.M. every Saturday there is a guided tour of Aix organized by the Tourist Office. Includes audiovisual presentation of Cézanne's life and oeuvre at the Granet Museum. Meeting point: Office du Tourisme, place du Général de Gaulle. Every Thursday during the tourist season the Tourist Office also offers a guided tour of Mont Sainte-Victoire, departing 2 P.M., returning 7 P.M. For general information and reservations call the Tourist Office at 33 (0) 4 42 161 161.

HOUSE OF DR. GACHET

78, rue du docteur Gachet, Auvers-sur-Oise.
In Auvers, the Tourist Office provides maps showing locations of important Cézanne motifs such as this house, where Cézanne received treatment for bouts of depression. The doctor's house and garden are open March 30 through October 30, from 2 P.M. to 6 P.M., closed Mondays.

United States

THE BARNES FOUNDATION

300 North Latch's Lane, Merion Station, PA 19066.
Major collection of Cézanne's art. Call for appointment: 215-677-0290.

CEDARIDGE FARM

Box 525, Pipersville, PA 18947.
Garden spaces inspired by Cézanne's garden. Visits by appointment only: 215-766-0699. Also view the website, www.derekfell.net.

OPPOSITE

View from the entrance to Cézanne's studio, Les Lauves, across the gravel courtyard to a flight of stone steps leading into the woodland garden.

129

Born and educated in England, Derek Fell has previously written books about the gardens of Renoir (*Renoir's Garden*), Monet (*Secrets of Monet's Garden*), and van Gogh (*Van Gogh's Gardens*), for which he received a best book award and best photography award from the Garden Writers Association. Married with three children, he lives at historic Cedaridge Farm in Pipersville, Pennsylvania, where he cultivates a series of award-winning theme gardens inspired by the great French Impressionist painters. A consultant on garden design to the White House during the Ford administration, Fell has lectured on the Impressionist painters at the Smithsonian Institution, the Barnes Foundation, the Philadelphia Museum of Art, and other art institutions.